LILLIAN TOO
JENNIFER TOO

ASTROLOGY & FENG SHUI

SHEEP 2018

IN THE YEAR OF THE EARTH DOG

KONSEPBOOKS

ASTROLOGY . FENG SHUI . INSPIRATIONS

FORTUNE & FENG SHUI 2018 SHEEP

by Lillian Too and Jennifer Too
© 2018 Konsep Lagenda Sdn Bhd

Published by KONSEP LAGENDA SDN BHD (223 855)
Kuala Lumpur 59100 Malaysia

For more Konsep books, go to www.lillian-too.com or www.wofs.com
To report errors, please send a note to errors@konsepbooks.com
For general feedback, email feedback@konsepbooks.com

ISBN 978-967-329-228-8
Published in Malaysia, August 2017

SHEEP 2018

Birth Year	Western Calendar Dates	Age	Kua Number Males	Kua Number Females
Metal Sheep	17 Feb 1931 – 5 Feb 1932	87	6 West Group	9 East Group
Water Sheep	5 Feb 1943 – 24 Jan 1944	75	3 East Group	3 East Group
Wood Sheep	24 Jan 1955 – 11 Feb 1956	63	9 East Group	6 West Group
Fire Sheep	9 Feb 1967 – 29 Jan 1968	51	6 West Group	9 East Group
Earth Sheep	28 Jan 1979 – 15 Feb 1980	39	3 East Group	3 East Group
Metal Sheep	15 Feb 1991 – 3 Feb 1992	27	9 East Group	6 West Group
Water Sheep	1 Feb 2003 – 21 Jan 2004	15	6 West Group	9 East Group
Wood Sheep	19 Feb 2015 – 7 Feb 2016	3	3 East Group	3 East Group

CONTENTS

uniquefengshui.com

CONTENTS

CHAPTER 6
SHEEP'S MONTH BY MONTH LUCK FOR 2018
Heaven luck bestows you with excellent instincts and good judgement

CHAPTER 1
Luck of the Sheep
in the Year of the Earth Dog 2018

LUCK OF THE SHEEP IN THE YEAR OF THE EARTH DOG

The Sheep enjoys a satisfying year when smart decisions lead to both small & big successes

In 2018, the sign of the Sheep receives heaven's blessings which combine brilliantly with its magnifying *Yi Duo Star*. This expands the impact of heaven luck star #6 that has flown into the Southwest sector. The #6 star is an auspicious white star and in 2018, it shines brilliantly, bringing unexpected windfalls and sudden opportunities.

It is also a very strong star in 2018 as it is supported by the Sheep's *Yi Duo Star,* so it is likely that the Sheep will benefit hugely from developments through the year. From this perspective, the Sheep is definitely having a good year.

The Sheep has the strength and life force to take fullest advantage of all that heaven's blessings bring, and this is an important factor when diagnosing the luck of the year for any sign. The Sheep has very good Windhorse luck – in other words, its personal *lung ta* is at a very good level. This means that its own capabilities and attitude to success will be very positive, and this will motivate the Sheep to reach for and attain some awesome goals.

> What is very encouraging also is that the Sheep is astrologically strong in this Dog Year, especially as it has the ally of the Rabbit, which makes two appearances in the year's Paht Chee chart.

This indicates that the Sheep has easy proximity to **friends and supporters** this year. It will hence be a relatively happy year when things work out well for you and your loved ones.

In terms of relationships, the Sheep who is single will very likely meet up with someone exciting who could send your heart strings zinging; while those already having partners or who are married will find new things to love about each other. The only problem for the Sheep this year is that your *spirit essence*, which enhances your instincts, are at low levels. This category of luck can diminish your enthusiasm and even cause you to occasionally feel depressed and bored with life. Here you need to use your inner strength to lift your own spirits. A high level of spirit essence is what sharpens your instincts and strengthens you. Because yours is low, you can find yourself occasionally feeling a pull towards being negative.

When you feel low and unappreciated this year, tell yourself there is no reason to indulge in this kind of self pity. What you can do to lift your spirits is to strengthen the **Earth element** near and around you.

Display **crystal** – balls, figurines, natural quartz points – and also if you can wear real gemstones, especially those surrounded by empowering mantras, this too will go a long way to magnifying your positive spirit essence.

Also, the Sheep should be smart when it comes to generating good feng shui energy for the year, as there are ways round any kind of element weakness in the chart.

The best way to ensure a good year is to move with the winds, so in 2018, it is a good idea to activate the #6 that has flown into your sector, the Southwest. Do this by creating powerful yang chi that causes frequencies of the #6 star to move and churn out good fortune vibrations.

ENERGIZING THE SOUTHWEST
Keep Southwest sector well-lit, play music here and rearrange your furniture so you spend time in this part of your room and of your home.

For some of you, like the **27 year old Metal Sheep** and the **63 year old Wood Sheep**, this can be a brilliant year that brings dramatic wealth luck. Both these Sheep are unlikely to lose money this year should you be investing in the markets. Those of you in commerce can count on your very strong success luck. Those involved in playing the share market can take a studied approach to making your investments work really well for you. Occasionally when you get a hot tip, and this is likely to be quite often this year, be brave, analyze carefully and then go for it.

Just make sure you do not over commit, don't get over-leveraged and for sure stay low key. This is the year of the yapping Dog and too much chatting about money matters can lead to problems.

The **75 year old Water Sheep** needs to be extra careful **about your health**. Avoid stress and reduce your socialising. Watch your spending this year and make certain not to live beyond your means. With Water being your heavenly stem, you will find the year quite dry indeed, as it is a year that lacks your producing element of Metal. The Paht

Chee chart indicates that the element of Metal is missing.

> The Sheep must be aware that the year's compass of 24 Mountains brings the winds of the *Yi Duo Star* into the location of the Southwest; where it signifies multiplying capability for you when matched with the Lo Shu square.

The good news is that in 2018, the 24 Mountains Compass also brings the Sheep the powerful *Star of Big Auspicious* facing the Sheep from the opposite sector. Here we see a situation where you can indeed parlay the #6 star energy to work strongly in your favour thereby manifesting something magical for you. The key here is to stay prepared and to consciously energize the Southwest with plenty of fresh yang chi.

The #6 star can bring some powerful transformations when it gets activated with the presence of vibrant yang chi energy. Yang energy gets created when there is bright light and movement, together with sounds of activity and life. So if you can work at making this happen in your Southwest sector, it will surely make a real difference.

You can also enhance your Southwest space with symbols of good fortune that directly activate the #6 star. If you want to generate **wealth vibrations**, place wealth symbols here such as the **Treasure Chests** and the **five Dzambhala images**. There are many different symbols of good fortune that bring enormous wealth luck, not least the **Wealth Deities**.

The Sheep's element profile for the year reveals the way its birth elements in the different luck categories interact with those of the year. This element luck profile calculation reveals the inner and outer luck for each of the 12 signs. It is an important chart to examine each New Year as they are a very accurate barometer of the way the luck cycles affect the quality of luck.

The Sheep's elements in 2018 look mixed. The most dominant trait that stands out in the chart is the strength of the Sheep's *lung ta*, which brings the luck of attaining what the Sheep sets out to do.

ELEMENT LUCK OF

2018	LIFE FORCE	HEALTH
WATER SHEEP 75/15 years	GOOD *O*	BAD *X*
WOOD SHEEP 63 years	GOOD *O*	**VERY GOOD** *OO*
FIRE SHEEP 51 years	GOOD *O*	NEUTRAL *OX*
EARTH SHEEP 39 years	GOOD *O*	**EXCELLENT** *OOO*
METAL SHEEP 87/27 years	GOOD *O*	VERY BAD *XX*

THE SHEEP IN 2018

	WEALTH	SUCCESS (LUNG TA)	SPIRIT ESSENCE
	VERY BAD *XX*	**VERY GOOD** *OO*	BAD *X*
	VERY GOOD *OO*	**VERY GOOD** *OO*	BAD *X*
	NEUTRAL *OX*	**VERY GOOD** *OO*	BAD *X*
	GOOD *O*	**VERY GOOD** *OO*	BAD *X*
	EXCELLENT *OOO*	**VERY GOOD** *OO*	BAD *X*

Your sign appears to have wonderful affinity with the mighty Windhorse, and when you display an image of either the **Windhorse,** or the powerful spiritual deity **King Gesar** himself riding the red Windhorse, this will ensure that ALL obstacles blocking the way to success get appeased.

Thankfully, the Sheep's life force is at a good level, hence the Sheep possesses the strength to overcome whatever negative aspects of your luck profile may manifest through the year. One way to ensure success luck never gets compromised is to carry the **Windhorse keychain,** which can also be used as a bag hanging by the ladies. There is also an amulet placed at the back of the Windhorse and this will give the Sheep's *spirit essence* a much-needed boost as well.

The Sheep benefits from inviting King Gesar riding his Windhorse into your home. This will lift the levels of your lung ta to help you achieve big success in 2018.

SHEEP'S 24 MOUNTAINS STARS

The Sheep's astrological location of SW1 has the magnifying star *Yi Duo* and this is excellent for the Sheep as the star #6 enters into the Southwest, while the other star also in the Southwest is the *Star of Golden Deity*. Thus both stars bring auspicious meanings that get strengthened and magnified by this star.

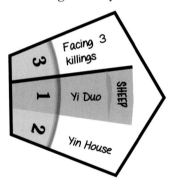

From across the Southwest, coming from the Northeast direction is the *Star of Big Auspicious,* and the way to bring this Big Auspicious Star into the Sheep's sector is to place this powerful **Peacock Mirror** in your Sheep location directly reflecting the Northeast direction.

The Peacock mirror has the *wishgranting mantra* placed round its frame, so it acts also like a wish-fulfilling mirror. Human energy will enhance the power of the mirror, thuis it helps to use your hands to hold the mirror to reflect the Northeast. And if there is a big auspicious symbol placed there, it will be even more effective.

Use the **oval mirror with colourful peacock** for all your big auspicious wishes related to worldly and material increases and use the **circular white peacock bejeweled mirror** to wish for big auspicious related to windfall luck that will elevate your status and position in the world. This is an incredibly powerful new spiritual tool that can also be used to actualize wishes when used as a personal feng shui prop.

Place the Peacock Mirror in the Sheep location of SW to benefit from the luck of Big Auspicious this year.

The White Peacock Bejewelled Mirror brings windfall luck. It will also increase Sheep's spirit essence, which is at a low ebb in 2018.

As the Sheep's spirit essence is at a low ebb, you can use the **White Peacock Mirror** to increase your spirit essence by reflecting the Monkey in the sector next to SW1 i.e. the SW3 sector and this is because the Monkey has excellent spirit essence in 2018. Using the reflective properties of the mirror in conjunction with powerful sanskrit wish granting mantras are a powerful dimension of feng shui as this takes us into the realms of the spiritual.

It is also a good idea to invite a replica of the **Bhoudanath Stupa of Katmandu**. With this Stupa in the home, you will be blessed by the iconic eyes of the Enlightened Ones on four sides of this magnificent Stupa. This ensures that you are never caught off guard in 2018.

Whatever afflictions may be coming from the four directions will be quickly and easily dissolved by the Stupa

Note that there are six powerful levels of spiritual protection associated with the Stupa, and its presence in any afflicted space is always very purifying. All worldly concerns are dealt with easily and effortlessly.

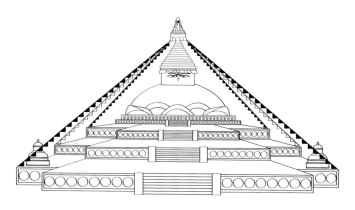

The Bhoudanath Stupa is an excellent energizer for the SHEEP in 2018. As well as enhancing all that is positive in your chart, it will protect against afflictions that may be directed your way.

This Stupa in the home will be strengthened by the presence of **Zangdok Palyri,** the **Mansion of the Lotus Buddha,** who is also known as Guru Rinpoche, which transforms the home into sacred space, causing the manifestation of the luck of *Big Auspicious* that is reflected into the Sheep sector from the NE direction.

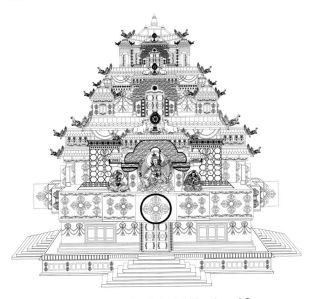

Zangdok Palyri, the Celestial Mansion of Guru Rinpoche, will transform your home into sacred space.

The *Star of Big Auspicious* always brings great good fortune to those who can capture its energies are sure to benefit from it. But to do so, the yang chi must be moving and brightly lit. Only then can the star actualize powerful good fortune to come your way. And with the Copper Mountain Mansion of Guru Rinpoche in the home, everything becomes incredibly auspicious for you in 2018.

PATRIARCHS AMONGST SHEEP-BORN

The Patriarchs amongst the Sheep-born can expect more good fortune to come his way. The good news of 2018 is that you benefit from the #6 star and in the Patriarch's corner of the compass, i.e. the Northwest sector of the home is another lucky star also a white star, that of #1 bringing strong victory to the Patriarch. Those amongst you Sheep who can add on the power of your strategic rituals of spiritual feng shui can create even more good fortune this year.

MATRIARCHS AMONGST SHEEP-BORN

The Matriarchs amongst Sheep-born meanwhile are doubly protected by the #6 star flying into the

Southwest sector of the year's chart. This means a doubling of the white star #6, an enormously positive number that brings vital assistance from heaven for all matriarchs of this sign. Note that for you, patronage comes from an unexpected quarter, so do not be surprised by goodwill shown to you from those you may not know well. This is the feature of the #6 star, which brings unexpected benefactor luck.

USE HO TU STAMP

To maximize the occurrence of the #1 and the #6 stars featuring so prominently in the patriarchal and matriarchal sectors of the compass, it is beneficial to use the *Ho Tu* combination of 1 and 6 stamps to generate another dimension of the 2018 luck profile.

All matriarchs and patriarchs can wear the **Prosperity Mantra Ring** and also add the **four Element Treasure Chests** on your work desk.

CHAPTER 2

LUCK OF THE
5 TYPES OF SHEEP

5 TYPES OF SHEEP

Heavenly Stem/ Earthly Branch	KUA Male/ Female	ASTROLOGY description
WOOD SHEEP **63 years (1955)**	**9E/6W**	Sheep works the land
FIRE SHEEP **51 years (1967)**	**6W/9E**	Sheep flies high
EARTH SHEEP **39 years (1979)**	**3E/3E**	Sheep in pasture
METAL SHEEP **27 years (1991)**	**9E/6W**	Sheep in business
WATER SHEEP **15 years (2003)**	**6W/9E**	Sheep in a flock

THE WOOD SHEEP
SHEEP WORKS THE LAND

Born in 1955
63 years old in 2018
Males are East group
Females are West group

PROSPECTS IN PERIOD 8:
Sheep builds big

PROSPECTS IN 2018:
Sheep on a roll

This Wood Sheep is the most hardworking and serious of those born under the sign of the Sheep. Your good fortune is that the harder you work, the greater is the success that comes your way. You also have great foresight and quite exceptional luck when it comes to working with the soil. Professions or businesses that involved agriculture or mining of the land will suit you very well. It is the land that will be the source of any big fortune you ultimately make. In the Period of 8, which is an Earth period, you will have benefitted from the energies of the Period enormously.

In 2018, this Sheep continues to enjoy a fabulous year. You are on a roll as luck is coming to you from all directions. There is wealth and health luck, and there is also success luck. Your lung ta is strong.

Those involved in commerce will see themselves achieving great strides in this Year of the Dog. You can take risks and you can also venture forth to other countries to expand your reach and your markets. But those involved in extracting minerals from the ground or planting in the Earth are strongly advised to offer incense daily to the Spirits of the Earth; this pacifies them and brings them onto your side. Also never forget to wear amulets daily, as your spirit essence this year is low.

The Wood Sheep has great foresight.

THE FIRE SHEEP
SHEEP FLIES HIGH

Born in 1967
51 years old in 2018
Males are WEST group
Females are EAST group

PROSPECTS IN PERIOD 8:
Sheep flies high

PROSPECTS IN 2018:
Looking to the skies

The Fire Sheep has tremendous
staying power.

The Fire Sheep is often the lone Sheep, the one who courageously strikes ahead of any pack to bring home the booty, and to build his family's fortunes often with great success. You have the fire of intelligence and you possess a burning ambition to make it big.

Many Sheep in this group do indeed succeed, and those who do not will never stop trying. This is because above all else, you have staying power and you have the stamina to keep going in pursuit of your ambitions. You are the personality that never gives up!

In 2018 the Year of the Dog, you carve out your own path. Your luck levels of wealth and health are at a neutral level, and what this means is that much depends on you yourself – how you respond to the way the year unfolds. But in terms of success luck, this you have in spades and it will help those of you who are intensely pursuing your vision hugely.

When one's *lung ta* is strong as yours is, then victory comes easily. Life becomes very joyous!

THE EARTH SHEEP
SHEEP IN PASTURE

Born in 1979
39 years old in 2018
Males and females are both EAST group

PROSPECTS IN PERIOD 8:
Sheep in pasture

PROSPECTS IN 2018:
Heaven fire burns bright

The Earth Sheep enjoys enormous energy in 2018.

The Earth Sheep is a Double Earth sign echoing that of the year 2018. This Sheep is positive and always encouraging, so you are never short of friends and helpful mentors. There is never a shortage of anything in your life and your pleasant disposition is contagious. The result is that during the Period of 8, an Earth Period, you will never be short of helpful friends and allies. This makes life very pleasant and you stay safe irrespective of what the outside environment may be manifesting for you and others.

In the year 2018, you have enormous energy. Your chi level is so good and although your spirit essence is at a low level, nevertheless, you have the stamina and staying power to attain some major successes this year.

THE METAL SHEEP
SHEEP IN BUSINESS

Born in 1991
27 years old in 2018
Males are EAST group
Females are WEST group

PROSPECTS IN PERIOD 8:
Sheep in business

PROSPECTS IN 2018:
Sheep on a roll

The Metal Sheep
meets with easy
success.

This is the Sheep most likely to succeed in business as you have the good fortune Commerce Star that creates the kind of understated luck that brings seemingly easy success. Behind the gloss however lies hard work and a great deal of determination. This is a Sheep who shuns the dramatic flourish of those who crave recognition and fame. The Metal Sheep prefers to play things very low key, staying humble in the face of even great success.

In 2018, this Sheep enjoys another outstanding year. There is excellent wealth luck and there is also easy success. Your lung ta is at a very good level, so the Windhorse of success blows fortunate winds your way. You do however need to take care of your health and those who may be in conflict with the Dog Year should install feng shui amulet cures.

Likewise, it is beneficial to enhance your spirit essence by burning incense daily. This will ensure you do not fall foul of naughty wandering spirits.

THE WATER SHEEP
SHEEP IN A FLOCK

Born in 2003
15 years old in 2018
Male is WEST group
Female is EAST group

PROSPECTS IN PERIOD 8:
Sheep in a flock

PROSPECTS IN 2018:
Strong success

The Water Sheep has a gentle nature.

The Water Sheep has a gentle nature that is often described as graceful; yours is a personality that is more suited to the arts than the sciences and many of you will excel in dance or music. Many people fall in love with you and it is unlikely that you are a one partner Sheep. Through your life you will enjoy more than one romantic encounter, and even in the past years during your youthful growing up years, whether you are a boy or girl, it is likely that you would have encountered romance already. Very young of course, so do be very careful.

In 2018, there is success luck in store for you over the next twelve months, but you need to be very careful in the way you commit to relationships. Remember that love is not a game to be played frivolously. There are always consequences to being foolish or careless. Better to focus on your studies this year, and in your friendliness, do be wary of sending out wrong signals that get misrepresented. Not much good can come from this.

CHAPTER 3
SIGNIFICANT HIGHLIGHTS
OF 2018
Year of the Earth Dog

SIGNIFICANT HIGHLIGHTS OF 2018
Year of the Earth Dog

The year 2018 calls for a shift in mindset. This is not a year to reap rewards or harvest the proceeds of things started in previous years. It is a year for consolidating what has already been started and focus on building and improving. It is a time that is beneficial for laying the groundwork for a grander, broader-based future. This is a year to think through and plan carefully before making decisions that affect your future, near or long term. Put your expertise and experience to good use, pause before acting. Refrain from being hasty.

For those about to set into the job market, adopt a posture of listening and learning. Taking this attitude will prevent you from jumping too quickly in new directions that might prove not to be optimum for you. Whatever the context of your situation as you read, this piece of advice applies very much in this Year of the Earth Dog.

It can be about connecting strongly with a love interest, moving into a new job, diversifying into new investments… whatever the context, be mindful not to make impetuous moves. This year, it will be the practical person that comes out best. Earth years always benefit those who take a pragmatic attitude towards career, work, love and life. They stay down-to-earth!

Patience yields the best outcomes. Whatever your situation, it is advisable to refrain from being impulsive. Always consciously make the effort to think things through and be mindful of taking risks. Consider very carefully before you change jobs, relocate, move house or start anything that requires a major change of pace or location. Even when it comes to matters of the heart, do not be hasty when making the big decisions.

In 2018, the key word to remember is "completion".

The way forward is to make sure you have completed everything begun previously before embarking on anything new. The key to success in 2018 is staying "still" so to speak. Rely less on instincts and more on sifting the facts from the fog that can cloud one's judgement. Do not get carried away by the illusion of resources you think you have. Indeed, there is no lack of capacity in 2018, but it is important to know that this can lead to over-confidence. Resources must be allocated properly to yield good outcomes.

If you think of this Year of the Earth Dog as being one of consolidation and preparation, a year to build and strengthen, you will be laying the groundwork for great success to come.

This is a year of **DOUBLE EARTH** – when the gregarious, loyal Dog offers plenty of opportunities to grow in many new directions, but the Dog Year this time around appears to lack the depth and inner essence to make things happen. Do not expect to see quick results to anything undertaken this year. Real effort and a lot of luck are required to make things happen. Yet many could be tempted into a comfort zone, and doing this could be dangerous. Those who lack experience must not get carried away just because there is no shortage of resources available.

This is a year when the abundance of resources needs to be used with creative thoughtfulness. Otherwise, resources and support can get wasted away. Success comes to those who are careful, patient and painstaking in their planning.

The year benefits those who have strong life force helping you. The **Ox, Tiger, Rabbit** and **Dragon** signs fall into this group, as do the **Sheep, Monkey, Rooster** and **Dog**. These eight signs will find that they have clarity of vision to truly get the best from the year. There will be effectiveness in your actions and your ideas yield productive results.

The second half of the year has a better outlook than the first half. The Pillars for the second half indicate a productive relationship of elements and many who have planned well through the year should see some quite spectacular results in the second half of the year. There is also a generally better outlook and good news at the end of the year.

The Water signs - **Rat** and **Boar** - need to work extra hard to energize themselves in 2018 due to their lacking the inner spirit and physical energy to blend harmoniously with the elements of the year. These signs need to strengthen their life force and inner essence. The effect of the Double Earth in the Year Pillar can also be stifling to these Water signs in terms of motivating them into getting galvanized to act.

Double Earth requires discipline, pragmatism and a down-to-earth attitude. All action must be well thought through. Logical and clear thinking are the keys to success. There is no room for impulsive action. Those who lack the vitality to get things done will find that they can get left behind. The element of Earth is a grounding element, so there must always be the input of practical and realistic thinking.

Note that despite this being a Double Earth year, there is also an excess of the Wood element, especially at the start of the year including February and March, indicating overcapacity and even a glut of resources and property.

The Paht Chee chart is UNBALANCED with missing Metal and excess Wood.

It is beneficial to go slow during the first two months of the year! This is not the time to make new investments or buy new property for investments.

BEST MONTHS FOR MAKING MONEY

In the twelve months from February 4th 2018 to February 3rd 2019, the best months in terms of wealth creation will be **August** and **September**. That is when the luck pillars are **Double Metal** for both months. The appearance of the Metal element will bring the winds that support all efforts at wealth creation – income wealth as well as asset wealth.

These two months benefit men in patriarchal or leadership positions. Those who have recently risen to high office or who were promoted last year, whether in Government or in Commerce, will feel the benefits of 2018's high energy chi blowing their way. Patriarchs enjoy the friendly buoyancy of benevolent winds and waters that translate into a positive flow of auspicious sum-of-ten luck followed by an abundance of good fortune.

They benefit from a special vitality that aids their judgment and decision-making. Luck improves, and the weakness of the first few months of the year gets dissolved. The lucky element of these months August and September is Metal.

Wear plenty of gold, or if you find this irksome, display auspicious and meaningful symbols made of metal and plated in gold. You will be sure to feel and see the difference!

FOR FINANCIAL LUCK:

Those wanting financial success, display a **Treasure Chest** overflowing with gold coins and gold ingots that symbolize powerful Metal element luck. Place this on your table in the NW sector of the desk. It can also be placed on a side cabinet in the NW sector of your office.

You can also use the set of **4 Dzambhala Treasure Chests** with each representing wealth from the Four Dakinis, each representing one of the four Enlightened families – the Jewel family, the Thunderbolt family, the Lotus family and the

Action family. Placed together, the 4 treasure chests of the four dakinis will bring exceptional wealth luck in these two special months of the year, and will be particularly beneficial to the patriarch of the family.

FOR SUCCESS LUCK:

Those wishing for your career luck to improve, especially those wanting promotions to manifest or those aiming for a particular position - to be made a partner, to be elevated to the Board or to be named to a particularly desirable position - should display the all-powerful **King Gesar riding the Wind Horse** with the banner of victory flying high. King Gesar's presence on your work table always signifies elevation to a higher position, sometimes even coming unexpectedly. Those in business wanting improvements in their sales or profits should call on King Gesar to bring the powerful winds of success their way. Either hang the Windhorse flag on the highest point of your home or work place, or display King Gesar's image on your desk. This sets up the energy of this wisdom protector, bringing you quite exceptional spiritual feng shui energies.

FOR ALL-ROUND HARMONY:

Those wanting their family or business to continue enjoying all-round success luck and smooth sailing through the year, it is an excellent idea to display an image of the **8 Immortals crossing the great waters** smoothly and safely. Better yet is to have this image lit up in the NW corner of your office or on your desk. The presence of the 8 Immortals is always auspicious, as they signify eight kinds of good fortune aspirations occurring smoothly for those who come under your care and guidance.

Indeed, once invited into any home, these powerful Immortals who signify the highest good of the Taoist teachings will always ensure that those who depend on you for their well-being will always enjoy smooth sailing in their endeavours. They bring a great deal of positive travel luck for the year, benefiting those amongst you who enjoy visiting new places and crossing the great waters.

MATRIARCHAL LUCK also manifests in September, and there will be a ripening of good news that benefits the family. This becomes exceedingly likely for those households who have invited in the image of the 8 Immortals into their living area. In the old days, a great many wealthy households of China will have artistic images of the 8 Immortals displayed in their homes either as works of art or in their porcelain collections.

The 8 Immortals are especially auspicious in this current Period of 8, and you will note that many Chinese artists add special lucky symbols into their art. When out shopping for an image of the 8 Immortals, make sure to look for the symbols of longevity - the crane, the pine tree and the peaches - and in addition, there is also the magical flute, the fan and the great Tai Chi symbol of yin and yang. We are making limited edition prints of a beautiful art piece of the 8 Immortals with all the important symbols available to those wanting to invite the 8 Immortals into their homes.

FOUR PILLARS OF DESTINY IN 2018

The Four Pillars chart that rule this Earth Dog Year of 2018 suggests a harmonious year dominated by the WOOD element. This indicates very strongly that pragmatism rules the energy of the year. This favours the establishment approach and it is not a good time to be rebellious towards authority. Indeed, it could be dangerous to go against the authorities or try to go against the law. Better to play the game according to the rules already set in place.

4 PILLARS CHART 2018

HOUR	DAY	MONTH	YEAR
癸 *Yin* **WATER**	丁 *Yin* **FIRE**	甲 *Yang* **WOOD**	卯 *Yang* **EARTH**
乙卯 *Yin* **WOOD** *Rabbit*	乙卯 *Yin* **WOOD** *Rabbit*	甲寅 *Yang* **WOOD** *Tiger*	戊戌 *Yang* **EARTH** *Dog*

The 2018 Paht Chee chart also reveals that the element of METAL, which stands for wealth and financial success, is missing from the main chart.

However, there is hidden Metal, and the element does make an appearance in the Luck Pillars of August and September. This indicates that in 2018, timing is of the essence in attaining wealth luck – it is missing from the main chart, so it is not easy to depend on wealth luck this year, but financial success can manifest during these two months.

Here are significant observations that emerge from this year's Paht Chee:

Firstly, the main chart lacks the METAL element, although there is one hidden Metal. Wealth creation can be described as missing. Whatever financial or wealth luck that manifests is indirect. Money-making opportunities will not be obvious or easy to identify. Metal appears strongly in August and September and it benefits the fathers of the family for both months and brings harmony luck to the mothers in September. Note however that this is a year of the double Earth, and this element creates the missing Metal energy.

So can anyone "create" wealth for themselves?

The answer is yes. Missing direct Metal signifies that what is thought to be lacking is available, but not obviously so. There is a preponderance of the Wood element and in 2018, this element represents support and resources available through the year. There are more than enough resources for whoever and whatever to create meaningful success! With a single Fire and single Water, both of which are yin, there is also creativity and power being exercised.

The year does not lack then for anything except that direct increases in prosperity will be harder to come by. There will be much less of the strident barking of the previous year, despite it being a Dog year.

The 2018 Dog is a mild and gentle loving creature!

Second, there are two yang pillars and two yin pillars, which bring wonderful yin and yang balance. Neither of the energy vortexes dominate. The presence of both yin and yang pillars ensures there is more than sufficient strength to propel the positive chi forward and upward. People in general are open to different viewpoints and are more prepared to live and let live.

Leaders pay greater respect to gender equality, and many of the negative energies that seemed so strident and loud in the past year will quiet down and be kept under control. Thus, the year moves forward on an even keel, thereby benefiting many. This reflects the greater balance of yin and yang, bringing more peace, and less strident rhetoric and divisiveness.

Third, the four Earthly Branches of the Pillars show two important affinities, with the Year Pillar of Dog forming a **secret friendship** with the Hour and Day Pillars of Rabbit. This means that there is a good beginning, a good in-between-time and a good ending to the year, what the Chinese refer to as having the head and having the tail, a suggestion that things can start with a very good chance of reaching more than a very satisfactory completion.

The two animal signs Dog and Rabbit are extremely harmonious. Both earthly branches possess the diplomatic skills to generate a year of good vibrations. There will be reduced anger energy in this year of the Dog, which endows the year with much-needed harmonious cooperation. There will be a big amount of live-and-let-live type mentality.

HOUR	DAY	MONTH	YEAR
癸 *Yin* **WATER**	丁 *Yin* **FIRE**	甲 *Yang* **WOOD**	卯 *Yang* **EARTH**
乙 卯 *Yin* **WOOD** *Rabbit*	乙 卯 *Yin* **WOOD** *Rabbit*	甲 寅 *Yang* **WOOD** *Tiger*	戊 戌 *Yang* **EARTH** *Dog*

The YEAR PILLAR of DOG forms a Secret Friendship with the HOUR and DAY PILLARS of RABBIT.

DOG and TIGER are Allies.

Note also that the Dog of the Year Pillar is in an **ally relationship** with the Tiger, and all that is needed to create even more loving energy during the year is the presence of the Horse. But the ally relationship of the Dog and Tiger bodes well for strategic alliances that get forged this year.

BOOST TIGER ENERGY

It will be extremely beneficial in 2018 to conjure up **Tiger energy** and keep the Dragon of the past year out of sight. For the feng shui of 2018, the White Tiger is more beneficial than the Green Dragon, as the Tiger is the ally of the Dog, while the Dragon is its astrological enemy. The White Tiger is a Protector, while the Tiger in general is always associated with Wealth Gods and Goddesses.

It really is beneficial to have the **Wealth God Tsai Shen Yeh** sitting on a Tiger placed in the living room, most preferably in the Northwest sector – the astrological home of the sign of the Dog. This actively brings the luck of wealth creation and makes up for the lack of the Metal element in the chart of the year. It is best to have it as a display image sitting on a mild looking benevolent Tiger. For those who want, they can also display the Hindu Goddess of Wealth Lakshmi sitting on a Tiger. This too is beneficial.

In 2018, it is extremely auspicious to invite into the home the Wealth God Tsai Shen Yeh sitting on a Tiger.

55

The Pillars also indicate that the year sees good communication between the different generations. There is a healthy respect from the young towards the older traditional values. This is an important signal as it bodes well for intra-family and inter-gender communications. This is indicated by the Rabbit in the Day and Hour Pillars having such a close relationship with the Year Dog Pillar. There is little danger then of there being discord this year. Greater understanding and tolerance is in the air, more so than in many previous years. This is a good indication for peace initiatives on the larger world stage to succeed.

This looks like it can be a peaceful Dog year, at least on the domestic front.

Fourth, there is strong authority luck, signified by the element of Wood, so a great deal of positive energy and authority will prevail in the world. The rule of law and good sense will triumph over hotheads and troublemakers. This indicates a maturing of the Period of 8, s uggesting that the world is getting tired of violence and angry energies.

The strong presence of the WOOD element in the year's chart indicates there are enough resources, and definitely sufficient support behind the rule of law and authority.

Feelings of rebelliousness and contentious opposition to the Establishment will likewise dissipate, although generally, the mood of nations and of families tend to be insular, i.e. looking inwards rather than outwards. The Wood element favours growth energy, a focus inwards and an attitude of being less intrusive into other people's affairs.

Fifth, there is *hidden* wealth luck, although this is not instantly obvious. Wealth luck in 2018 is indirect and it must be activated to manifest. Those who want to can (and should) enhance their wealth luck element of 2018, which is to bring the element of Metal into their homes to make up for the missing Metal from the main Paht Chee chart of the year.

> Note that the Wealth element for the year (which applies to everyone) is METAL and there are many ways to enhance this.

Different animal signs will benefit in different ways of course, but generally, simulating GOLD in the home benefits households strongly in terms of generating wealth luck. Thus gold-coloured curtains and décor are beneficial and anything metallic is favourable. It is also extremely fortunate if you already have a Deity of Wealth in your home ensuring your household will enjoy a continuation of prosperity, but if you do not have such a deity, it is beneficial to invite in a Wealth Deity.

Six, there is one potentially very auspicious star in the year's Four Pillars chart. This can bring good fortune to those who know how to activate and energize it correctly, simultaneously ensuring the positive aspects of its influences materialize.

The lucky star of the year is the *Commanding Star*, an outstandingly auspicious star to have in the year's chart, and it benefits ambitious people the most. The higher you aim for, the more spectacular your success will be. This is because it indicates the presence of authority, power and influence favouring such people strongly. In Chinese, this star is named *Jiang Sin*, or the Commanding Star.

This star bestows charisma on those who have the courage to stand out and aim for great things. It benefits those in leadership positions, bestowing on them the potential to become heroes, giving them an easy air of authority as if they are somehow born to rule. Note however that you need to wear a **special amulet** to strongly manifest the good fortune attributes of the *Commanding Star*.

This star brings wealth and recognition, and causes many people to follow and respect you. It favours powerful political leaders, or CEOs of companies and organizations. To succeed and enjoy the patronage of this star in 2018, the first step is to generate the desire and determination to succeed. It benefits those who have the ambition and the staying power to move strongly forward in whatever they may be engaged in.

The Commanding Star bestows great charisma and admiration, and public success. But in 2018, this star has to be activated, as the lack of Metal in the year's chart causes this star to lose strength.

The only problem with this star is that while it is an excellent star, unfortunately in 2018, the element of Metal is missing. This causes the star to lose strength.

As such, we have created the **Commanding Star Amulet** in Metal to ensure that the positive aspects of this most auspicious star can manifest strongly in your favour. Those who do not activate this star are unlikely to benefit from the benefits of its appearance in the year's chart. Those enjoying obvious good fortune, those on a roll this year must remember to go easy on their impatience. They need to make extra effort to curb their impulsive and even arrogant behaviour.

Be careful not to ride roughshod over competitors. Temper all major decisions with wisdom and make sure that whatever afflictions affect your animal sign are properly suppressed with the right remedies. Otherwise you can easily waste away the good chi of this excellent star.

WEALTH LUCK IN 2018

This year of the Earth Dog is lacking in wealth luck. The annual energies of the year do not favour making money. Hence it is helpful to invite the image of Wealth Gods into your home.

The sign of the SHEEP is associated with the powerful Wealth Goddess who brings a multiplication of whatever wealth you already have or may have inherited. The sign of good fortune for the Sheep is also the deer that brings longevity and is often drawn with the God of Longevity known as "Sau". Having his image either alone or with two other Taoist Gods to create the Trinity of Fuk Luk Sau is extremely auspicious for the home. More so, in terms of ensuring wealth luck, if you also invite into the home the five Dzambhalas or Wealth Gods in five colours signifying the five elements. Place the Yellow Dzambhala in the center for best impact. Also invite in the Lord of the Wealth Gods, the great Guardian King of the

North to ensure that your household will always have its wealth safeguarded.

There is a powerful wealth-bringing ritual involving the placement of **four wealth chests** offered to the White Dzambhala by the four offering goddesses that can bring incredible wealth luck to households, and for Sheep who wants to spurt ahead in 2018, they can consider performing this wealth ritual.

Invite all five Wealth Dzambalas into your home. They will bestow great wealth luck to all in the household.

Note that in 2018 it is extremely beneficial to invite a Wealth God or the complete set of five Enlightened Family Dzambhalas into the home. These bring the accumulations of five element chi, which is so powerful for creating new prosperity. Those who have already amassed some asset wealth (property, businesses etc) can invite the Lord of the Yakshas NAM TOSE, who as one of the Four Great Kings, safeguards the wealth of families and households.

Finally, note that the Tiger has good affinity with the Dog Year, so allowing the Tiger to bring in the Wealth God *Tsai Sheng Yeh* (who sits on the Tiger) is also appropriate, as the affinity of these two signs magnifies the auspicious presence of the Taoist Wealth God.

For self-enhancement of wealth luck, wear or carry in your hand bag our **wealth-enhancing amulets** to strengthen the prosperity aura created by the Wealth Gods and the Dzambhalas that have been invited into your home.

GET A NEW WEALTH WALLET

An auspicious ritual to strengthen wealth luck each year is to get a NEW wealth wallet and then to ensure a continuity of good fortune, you should transfer some old money into the new wallet. To welcome fresh prosperity, you must also place new money into the wallet. If someone "gives" you lucky money during the 15 days of the Lunar New Year or if you have money given to you from a wealthy man's pocket, place this into your wallet to absorb their wealth energy into your aura.

One of the best ways to start the new year right is to invest in a brand new wealth wallet. When you start using it, always transfer some money over from your old wallet, and also add in NEW money.

WHITE COLOUR IS LUCKY FOR 2018

In 2018, the METAL element is the most important element, so the best colour to strengthen and broaden around you is white with a metallic tinge. Enhancing white light around you not only strengthens wealth luck, it also strengthens your life force.

WEALTH TALISMANS FOR THE YEAR

In 2018 everyone benefits from carrying the **wealth amulet of the year**. The best talisman to attract wealth and prosperity in 2018 is to wear the **King Gesar Mantra Ring**.

Amulets that incorporate powerful mantras and seed syllables are best worn close to the body touching the skin at chakra or energy points wherever possible. Wearing them as rings, pendants or bracelets are extremely empowering. Amulets can also be kept inside wallets or worn as hangings on bags, or they can be placed above bedroom doorways.

King Gesar Mantra Ring to attract wealth and prosperity.

There are also special talismans that benefit each of the four groupings of allies, and in each of these bespoke talismans, there is an image and mantra that has special affinity to the grouping of three allies.

Those born in years of the Rabbit, Boar and Sheep should have the wishfulfilling jewel pendant with symbols of the excellent Stack of Auspiciousness Sutra hung alongside it.

The Sheep benefits from wearing the wishfulfilling jewel pendant with Stack of Auspiciousness Sutra hung alongside it.

CHAPTER 4

THE FENG SHUI CHART OF 2018

THE FENG SHUI CHART OF 2018

When it comes to the management of one's astrology luck and feng shui, it is all about good timing and placement. When you get the scheduling of your decisions right and the execution of your actions can proceed with few obstacles, the chances of success are definitely improved. The probability of events and outcomes working out according to your wishes are then more certain to go your way.

In fact, when you speak to high achievers in any field, they will acknowledge that good timing definitely plays a crucial part in their ongoing success. It is also necessary to note the month to month updates that enable you to cope with the high and low tides of luck.

It is always beneficial to stay up to date on your astrological outlook and the time dimension of feng shui, which requires you to study and understand the Feng Shui Chart of 2018. These reveal the feng shui afflictions of your living and work spaces which need then to be treated with feng shui cures. These remedies are vital and we pride ourselves on the great authenticity of those that we make. We are strict on design and quality control because we know how important is the energy "attached" to feng shui cures.

Similarly, the lucky sectors of this year must also be energized with the correct placement of the luck enhancers according to the year's annual chart. When good fortune sectors and stars are properly energized, they bring amazing good fortune. The household's overall luck is also sure to be immediately improved. Our books, cures and enhancers have grown in popularity over the past 18 years simply because they work so well for so many people, helping them avoid misfortune luck, and to live far better lifestyles than they could ever have imagined.

Staying updated on the feng shui of the year means insulating yourself from severe reversals of fortunes. When you are not protected, you do become vulnerable to the intangible killing energies that come your way during bad months, and the misfortune, betrayal or illness that hits can sometimes strike so hard as to even spill over to affect your good months.

Remember that bad things can happen to good people, and since it does not require much effort to be guarded against the bad luck energies of the year, it is absolutely worthwhile to do so – whether or not you believe in it.

In 2018, it is just as important to position yourself favourably to receive all the good luck the year promises.

UNLOCKING THE YEAR'S ENERGY PATTERNS

The Feng Shui chart should be viewed as a key to recognizing the energy patterns of the year. When correctly analyzed, sectors of any building that are afflicted by bad energy numbers can be quickly identified, and also rectified. Likewise, the luckiest parts of buildings can also be ascertained and enhanced.

The Flying Star chart of the year can be superimposed onto homes and offices alike, and using the compass to anchor the kind of affliction/auspicious luck of the different rooms and corners enables feng shui remedies/activators to be put into place.

As you read about the eight sectors of your home (use a compass to mark out the spaces then put in place all the notes you are making as you read this book. It is good to systematically take notes of the energy pattern for the year. Invest in a reliable compass and then correctly move from room to room to remedy the afflictions of rooms within and also enhancing the auspicious sectors as recommended.

FLYING STAR CHART 2018

8	4	6
Prosperity **Southeast**	*Peach Blossom* **South**	*Heavenly Star* **Southwest**
7	9	2
Violence **East**	*Completion* **Center**	*Illness* **West**
3	5 *Three Killings*	1 *Tai Sui*
Quarrelsome **Northeast**	*Five Yellow* **North**	*Victory Luck* **Northwest**

Here we use the feng shui and astrological charts
to generate the analysis. It is like diagnosing
the troublesome areas that can lose you money,
cause you misfortune, add to your daily stress and
worries, and identifying good luck sectors that
have the potential to bring you great happiness
and wealth when correctly activated. And then
we use physical objects that symbolize Element
cures and enhancers to improve the feng shui.

LUCKY & UNLUCKY SECTORS

Feng shui updates ensure the continuation of
good feng shui, so we devote a section exclusively
on the changing chi energy patterns for the New
Year. These are conveniently laid out so it is easy
for you to take remedial actions by correctly
placing cures to dissolve bad energy in afflicted
sectors.

All houses are affected by the energy patterns that
change every year. You may have benefited from
good chi last year, but things are likely to have
changed in 2018. One example is the energy of
the North, which in 2017 benefited from heaven
luck, but in 2018 gets hit by the misfortune-
bringing star, the *Five Yellow.*

Auspicious enhancers should also be placed to strengthen the new lucky corners of 2018, as this adds to the flow of good fortune coming into the home space. This practice of Time Feng Shui helps you stay protected and ensures you can maximize your personal luck as well as the luck of your home.

This year, **Southeast-facing houses** enjoy good luck, as do **Northwest-facing houses**, which receive good chi from sitting Southeast. The Southeast benefits from the number 8 star and the Snake direction of Southeast 3 is aided by the 24 Mountains *Star of Heavenly Seal*. This brings good fortune to those born in Snake years.

SE and NW facing houses are particularly lucky in 2018.

The Northwest enjoys the white star number 1, which brings victory and is aided by the 24 Mountains *Star of Small Auspicious*, which manifests a series of good fortune events benefiting those born in the years of the Dog and Boar. Note however that the Boar is afflicted by the *Robbery Star,* also brought by the 24 Mountains.

Do understand that everyone benefits from safeguarding their homes and work places from the afflictions of the year simply because these afflictions brought by the Flying Star Chart and the 24 Mountains chart can sometimes be deadly. They can sometimes cause serious reversals of fortune that have disastrous consequences for the family, which can be far reaching in their impact. It is always beneficial to make the effort to update your feng shui each year.

All you need to know is where and how strong the afflictions of the New Year are, get them subdued and be assured of a safe and smooth passage through the year. Being forewarned is forearmed, because the remedies are easy to use when you know what to do. Cures and enhancers are powerful in their effect on your lives in 2018.

FENG SHUI CHART OF THE YEAR OF THE EARTH DOG 2018

Heaven Seal

	Snake 🐍	Horse 🐎	Sheep 🐐	
Dragon 🐉	**8** Prosperity Southeast	**4** Peach Blossom South	**6** Heavenly Star Southwest	Monkey 🐿
Rabbit 🐇	**7** Violence East	**9** Completion Center	**2** Illness West	Rooster 🐓
Tiger 🐅	**3** Quarrelsome Northeast	**5** Five Yellow North	**1** Victory Luck Northwest	Dog 🐕
	Ox 🐂	Rat 🐀	Boar 🐗	

Big Auspicious — Dragon side

Golden Deity — Monkey side

Earth Seal — Tiger side

Tai Sui — Dog side

Big Auspicious

Small Auspicious

3 Killings

75

THIS YEAR'S NUMBER IS 9

The Feng Shui chart is created using the Lo Shu number of the year. This year's number is 9 and in addition to using this number to create the chart by placing 9 in the center, 9 is also regarded as the lucky number of the year.

With 9 in the center, the chart's distribution of numbers generates the sum of 18 (which also add up to 9 when we add the two digits together) then adding any three numbers that cut across the center vertically, horizontally or diagonally.

This is hugely significant as it underlines the all-pervasive influence of 9 this year. 9 is also the number that symbolizes Future Prosperity in this current Period of 8, and 9 is the number of Completion. The year's number itself is 9 (signifying the completion of the first cycle of 9 numbers for this new century).

In Chinese numerology, 9 is the ultimate number. According to Flying Star analysis, the number 9 is an auspicious number with a multiplying effect. Good becomes better, while bad becomes worse. Since the year 2018 is a genial year of the peaceful Dog, the influence of 9 is read as being very good indeed – in a most positive way.

Feng shui experts of the Far East acknowledge that 9 is in many ways more potent even than 8, although of course together, the combination is unbeatable, as it means current and future prosperity.

So 9 in the period of 8 is very significant. The improvement of anyone's feng shui in 2018 cannot ignore the power of 9. It should be incorporated into the symbolic enhancers for the year.

Multiples of 9 must feature prominently in anything placed with a view to energizing space or personal auras. Thus nine rod wind-chimes, nine fish in an aquarium, nine charms in a bracelet, nine levels of flow in a water feature, nine coins and nine currencies in wealth vases and so forth would be extremely beneficial in multiplying the good effects.

The number 9 is also the Lo Shu number of babies born in this year of the Dog. There are of course personality characteristics associated with the Lo Shu number that one is born with. the #9 here brings future prosperity for those who are going through their first cycle of life.

THE FENG SHUI CHART OF 2018

The Feng Shui chart with 9 in the center shows the other eight numbers that occupy the eight sectors of the chart. This chart can be applied to any building based on the compass demarcation of primary and secondary directions.

Around the chart are the animal signs placed according to their individual house location on the compass. Included also are the lucky auspicious stars of the 24 mountains. This chart summarizes the more significant information needed to "read" the year for each of the twelve signs, and to read the luck of houses based on their compass orientations.

Those who want additional information on the energy patterns of the year can also refer to our annual FENG SHUI ALMANAC calendar, where we have compiled all the most relevant information needed for modern living, including good and bad days (and hours) to perform key tasks such as opening a new business, starting renovations, moving house, getting married and signing important contracts.

The analysis of the feng shui chart involves assessing the strength of the numbers in the different sectors. We investigate how they are influenced by the "lucky stars" brought by the 24 mountains (i.e. sub-directions) that appear to benefit some of the animal signs more than others. These influence the astrological fortunes of the animal sign and the different compass sectors of houses.

Understanding these different stars and numbers and their interaction with the intrinsic elements of the sectors and the animal signs collectively unlocks significant things about the year for each sign. This enables the knowledgeable practitioner to really get the best from the analysis.

This seamless merging of Chinese zodiac astrology with feng shui is simplified into an easy-to-understand context, and it is this that brings excellent value to these little books, which we research, compile and write every year. This is the 18th year of this series of Astrology & Feng Shui books. Each year, we delve a little deeper into the influences that affect the fortunes of the twelve animal signs. We also share powerful feng shui recommendations that address the positive and negative aspects of the luck as revealed in the numbers and compass sectors of the charts.

The reader can use the analysis in this section to move from sector to sector within their homes and from room to room, systematically installing symbolic and other feng shui remedies affected by bad chi energy; and placing the powerful activating enhancers to strengthen the good luck corners.

THE #9 IN THE CENTER

This brings positive frequencies to everyone, as the power of 9 pervades all buildings, homes and offices throughout the year.

This number, which indicates future prosperity, sets the tone for the best attitude to adopt in 2018, and that is to build for the future. The number 9 is indicating that the seeds for building future prosperity can be sown this year by creative, courageous and ambitious people. Their efforts are sure to bear fruit, although there are variations to the timing of when each sign's harvest time can be.

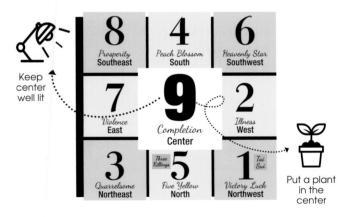

Keep center well lit

Put a plant in the center

8 *Prosperity* **Southeast**	4 *Peach Blossom* **South**	6 *Heavenly Star* **Southwest**
7 *Violence* **East**	9 *Completion* **Center**	2 *Illness* **West**
3 *Quarrelsome* **Northeast**	5 *Three Killings* *Five Yellow* **North**	1 *Tai Sui* *Victory Luck* **Northwest**

The only thing about 9 in the center is that this is a Fire number flying into an Earth sector. The energy of 9 in the center of the house is described as getting exhausted. That it is also a Double Earth year makes it even more exhausting.

To counter this, the Fire element in the center of buildings must be strengthened. Keep this part of any home well lit, especially if the dining area is located here. The Paht Chee chart meanwhile is indicating a surplus of Wood, and this produces Fire. Though the 9 is being used up, it is also being constantly revitalized!

Install a **new chandelier** or place **light activators** to ensure a flow of creative luck for the future. Another way is to expand the number of lights here or to increase the wattage of light bulbs. Remember that 9 is a powerful number, so replenishing and activating it is

extremely beneficial. Placing plants here can also help as the Wood Element fuels the Fire.

The placement of a spiritually-enhanced symbol to bring out the special significance of the Flying Star #9 bringing Completion Luck is the placement of the **Nine Golden Pears** together with **Zangdok Palyri,** the sacred Pure Land of Guru Rinpoche's Copper Mountain. This will set the foundation for an incredibly prosperous future for all who bring this Pure Land Mansion into their homes.

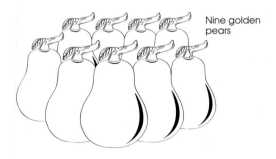

Nine golden pears

SUBDUING ILLNESS STAR IN THE WEST

The illness star 2 flies to the West in 2018. It resides in the place of the Metal Element – so Earth flies into Metal. On the surface, this causes the illness star to get weakened, so it would appear like it does not pose serious danger to those whose bedroom is in the West, or whose main doors are facing the West.

However, the West is also the place of the trigram TUI, which stands for "the lake", indicating the essence of Water Element, and since Earth is dominant over Water, the Trigram is weakened by

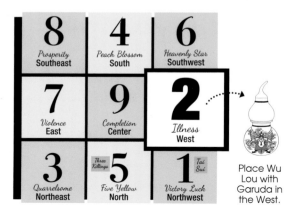

8	4	6
Prosperity **Southeast**	*Peach Blossom* **South**	*Heavenly Star* **Southwest**
7	9	2
Violence **East**	*Completion* **Center**	*Illness* **West**
3	5	1
Quarrelsome **Northeast**	*Three Killings* *Five Yellow* **North**	*Tai Sui* *Victory Luck* **Northwest**

Place Wu Lou with Garuda in the West.

the illness star 2. This creates a hazardous threat, as the danger brought by the illness star is hidden.

The correct remedy is needed to suppress the illness star, and while a **brass wu lou** is always effective as a remedy, this hidden affliction being more dangerous because it is not obvious needs to be addressed. This is why we have made some subtle but powerful additions to the wu lou, which are the image of the powerful Garuda to suppress the nagas that bring illness.

The addition of the gemstone is to symbolize the wish-granting jewel that is the Medicine Buddha. Placed in the West, this special brass wu lou will totally suppress the star of 2 and also suppress the *Star of Reducing Energy,* as well as the *Yearly Conflict Stars* brought by the 24 Mountains Compass.

The West is also the astrological location of the sign of the Rooster and in 2018, those born under this sign will benefit from wearing this beautiful **Wu Lou pendant**, which is like a mini version of the remedy you can place in your sector. Those sleeping in bedrooms in the West can also wear the Wu Lou as a safeguard against illness in 2018.

1 Keep lights at the front door dim to avoid strengthening the number 2 star.

2 Place metal **Wu Lou** and windchimes in the foyer area to suppress the illness star.

THINGS TO DO IN 2018 IF YOU LIVE IN A **WEST-FACING HOUSE OR A WEST-LOCATED ROOM**

3 If there are young girls in the house, place **Buddha Acala** in their room.

4 Place a special **Wu Lou with garuda** symbol in the West part of living area.

5 Paint the door or wall in the West white to keep the 2 star suppressed.

#3 QUARRELSOME STAR IN NORTHEAST

The noisy, quarrelsome star 3 flies to the Northeast, bringing hostile energy and problems associated with arguments, fights, misunderstandings and court cases to residents residing here.

The number 3 star is capable of making small problems BIG thereby creating unnecessary aggravations that turn serious. Unfortunately for anyone having a bedroom in the Northeast sector of the house, the hostile star 3 is strong this year

8 Prosperity Southeast	4 Peach Blossom South	6 Heavenly Star Southwest
7 Violence East	9 Completion Center	2 Illness West
3 Quarrelsome Northeast	5 Three Killings Five Yellow North	1 Tai Sui Victory Luck Northwest

Display pair of red and gold tzi chi dogs in the NE.

because its intrinsic Wood Element dominates the Earth energy of the Northeast.

However, those who reside in the Tiger sector of Northeast 3 sector will feel the influence of the fearsome 3 a lot more. The Tiger is by nature an aggressive animal of the wilds, and when it gets activated by the number 3 star, it generates aggressive energy, so those whose rooms are here will be more seriously affected by the quarrelsome vibes of the number 3 star.

What is potentially more dangerous is that the Tiger is also affected by the 24 Mountains Star of *Earth Seal*, so chi energy of the NE3 has the potential to be very stealthy indeed.

The 3 star is a Wood element star, and the traditional way of overcoming this is to exhaust it with Fire Element. Anything that suggests Fire is an excellent cure, so **all kinds of lights** and the **colour red** are suitable remedies here. Last year when the #3 star afflicted the West sector, it brought a great deal of anger energy directed at President Trump and this was due to the West Wing of the White House getting hurt by this star. This year, the #3 star is in the NE sector, where the # 3 star is less strong than it was last year. Nevertheless, it is always advisable to keep it under control as it can create havoc for those whose inner essence is weak.

In our research on this matter, we have created a **special incense burner/container,** which you can use to make regular incense offerings to the local spirits who reside in this sector of your home. This should go a long way to appeasing whatever quarrelsome or litigious energy that may arise to cause you annoyance and problems. The incense offering will also prevent small misunderstandings growing into large problems.

If you like, you can also display a **red and gold Tzi Chi Dog** made of brass and metal to suppress the #3 star in the NE this year. For a simpler solution to the #3 star, displaying a **bowl of red apples** in the home's NE sector can be remarkably effective.

1 Do not place water near the front door as this strengthens the number 3 star.

2 Place **Manjushri's Flaming Red Sword** on a console table facing the main door.

THINGS TO DO IN 2018 IF YOU LIVE IN A NORTHEAST-FACING HOUSE OR A NORTHEAST-LOCATED ROOM

3 Turn on the lights at the front of the house and keep foyer area well lit.

4 Paint the door or a wall here red to keep the number 3 star suppressed.

5 Place water at the back of the house to activate the Indirect Spirit of the SW.

#4 PEACH BLOSSOM IN THE SOUTH

The South was very afflicted last year. This year 2018, the sector comes out of it and is graced by the presence of a *Peach Blossom Star* bringing the luck of literacy and romance. This is signified by the number 4, which is regarded also as a love star considered lucky for singles and unmarried people, but is viewed with suspicion for those already married.

Placing Horse images in the South brings marriage luck in 2018.

8 Prosperity Southeast	4 Peach Blossom South	6 Heavenly Star Southwest
7 Violence East	9 Completion Center	2 Illness West
3 Quarrelsome Northeast	5 Three Killings Five Yellow North	1 Tai Sui Victory Luck Northwest

Peach Blossom luck is often associated with infidelity, and older married people do not like it when it flies into their bedroom! So if your room is in the South and you are married, it might not be a bad idea to symbolically distill its influence with bright lights that bring Fire energy, which works for marriages. This prevents either husband or wife succumbing to temptation to go outside the marriage for sexual gratification.

Unmarried people who want to activate their marriage and romance luck can do so with the presence of Water. In 2018, the Peach Blossom aspect of the number 4 is weak because it is in the South, so its Wood energy will get strengthened with the presence of water... but not too much, as the texts also warn against too much water when Peach Blossom energy is present.

Here in the South, the romance star favours women who are getting along in age and still single. Those keen on enhancing marriage luck must activate your Peach Blossom luck by placing images of Horses in the South. As 2018 is a Dog Year, placing a Horse in the South benefits everyone's inner Peach Blossom for the year.

In the South location this year, the #4's literary side is also strong, bringing **study and academic luck** to those residing in this part of their home.

The South sector generically stands for attainment and recognition, so with an auspicious number having flown here, those whose good luck are associated with the South direction (or if they are East group people) should make the most of it in 2018.

If you occupy this part of your house, be mindful of this. Depending on the kind of attainment you wish for, you can enhance the sector with a relevant symbolic feng shui enhancer here.

The number 4 is advantageous for those engaged in the writing profession. So if you are employed in writing as a career or you are in research, in the media or involved in any kind of academic pursuits, staying in the South or enhancing its chi energy with **bright lights** is certain to attract recognition for you in these areas this year. Display the **bejeweled Wind Horse** in the South and let it enhance the Peach Blossom in 2018. The Wind Horse is always associated with success-bringing frequencies.

The Wind Horse is an excellent feng shui activator for the South sector in 2018, bringing success energies, especially in the field of education, examinations and also in love and romance.

1 Enhance the foyer and front area of your house with bright lights.

2 Enhance the South with red flowers such as hibiscus, peonies or bougainvilleas.

THINGS TO DO IN 2018 IF YOU LIVE IN A SOUTH-FACING HOUSE OR A SOUTH-LOCATED ROOM

3 Keep lights turned on through the night, as this is particularly auspicious.

4 Those wanting love should hang a painting of nine horses facing the door.

5 A symbolic writing brush on the ledge above the main door brings scholastic luck.

#5 WU WANG STAR IN THE NORTH

The Five Yellow or *wu wang* flies to the North in 2018, bringing danger of misfortune to anyone who occupies a room here. The Five Yellow can create havoc in the lives of those afflicted by it. If your bedroom or front door – the door you use the most – are located here, it can bring you distress and misfortune.

This is a situation that is viewed with nervousness by anyone familiar with feng shui, and because it

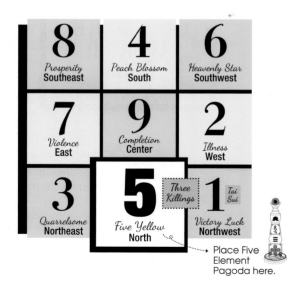

8	4	6
Prosperity **Southeast**	*Peach Blossom* **South**	*Heavenly Star* **Southwest**
7	9	2
Violence **East**	*Completion* **Center**	*Illness* **West**
3	5 *Three Killings*	1 *Tai Sui*
Quarrelsome **Northeast**	*Five Yellow* **North**	*Victory Luck* **Northwest**

Place Five Element Pagoda here.

is an Earth element number, it easily dominates the North's Element of Water. Definitely, the cure needs to be strong and powerful.

Everyone should try to suppress the pernicious effects of this afflictive number. The influence of the Five Yellow can spread to other parts of the house unless remedies are put into place in the North sector of the house or office. Note that this is a year of Double Earth, so stronger measures are called for because the Five Yellow is an Earth Element star.

Usually in the current Period of 8 (an Earth Period) the Five Element Pagoda would be strong enough to ward off its bad effects, but because Earth chi is so strong in 2018, the Five Yellow remedy must be more powerful than usual, and better yet, it should rise from water as it is in the water sector in the North.

The most powerful remedy for the 2018 wu wang Five Yellow is the Be-jeweled Five Element Pagoda with sun, and which arises from water.

The most powerful remedy for the *wu wang* is the **Bejeweled Five Element Pagoda** topped by a bejeweled sun and which arises from water. The square base has the powerful Double Dorje, and the seed syllable Hum has also been placed on four sides of the pagoda to dispel all other dark forces that may be hovering near the wu wang.

Place this pagoda remedy in the North sector of the living room. If you have several levels in your home, it is beneficial to place one pagoda on each level. The remedy for the Five Yellow is always made of brass and is filled with powerful dispelling mantras that bring peace and harmony into the home.

Another powerful cure that can dispel all dark forces associated with the Five Yellow and other bad forces is the incredibly powerful remedy known as the **8 Hums Protection Wheel**. If you have an altar in your home, place this on the altar. Otherwise, place it high on a side cabinet. This feng shui cure brings wonderful vibrations into the home and its presence will ensure that all hostilities are appeased.

This remedy can suppress any ongoing misfortune luck, or if you or your family are going through really tough times associated with broken relationships or loss of income streams (such as losing your job) or a particularly bad illness, then you can boost your feng shui efforts with this powerful remedy.

Unless suppressed, the Five Yellow can cause severe illness, accidents and loss in many aspects of life. Sometimes, just facing the Five Yellow direction can bring ill luck of some kind.

The Five Yellow is the catalyst for bringing various manifestations of misfortune. It can cause your life to suddenly collapse around you. When you read about tragedies striking a family, you can be sure that the Five Yellow is somehow responsible, either because it afflicts the main door or the bedroom that the victim occupies.

If your main door, your bedroom or even your office desk is afflicted by the Five Yellow, due to their location in the North, the affliction must be dealt with before 4th February 2018.

Do not be careless or forget about it, as bad luck caused by the Five Yellow can manifest quickly. When it does, it might be too late to do something about it. Prevention is better than cure, so do not wait until it is too late. You must also check where the Five Yellow flies to each month.

Those born in the **Sheep** year must be extra careful in the month of **AUGUST** as this is the month when the Five Yellow also flies into your month chart. This is when you must be protected from the Five Yellow, so carry the **Pagoda Hanging** to ward off bad luck associated with this affliction.

Misfortune caused by the Five Yellow in 2018 can be severe business loss or threatening terminal illness. Antidotes must be put into place. Houses that face South require one or both of the remedies suggested. This is because houses that face South are deemed to be sitting North.

Here, the Five Element Pagoda and the 8 Hums Protection Wheel are especially powerful for warding off problems. Place the remedies at the back of the house. This should shield the home from the killing energies of these afflictions.

If you reside in a room located in the North, you need to place the cure inside your room. Do the placement of cures at the start of the year. The Five Yellow Pagoda of the previous year can be placed on your altar. The remedy for this year should be placed in the North sector of the living room or the home. The new cure is needed to make the energies fresh.

OVERCOMING THE THREE KILLINGS

The North is also afflicted by the Three Killings in 2018. This is a phenomenon that affects only primary directions. The Three Killings bring three types of severe misfortune associated with loss, or destruction of good fortune. Its location each year is charted according to the animal sign that rules the year. This year it flies to the North, because the Dog belongs to the Triangle of Affinity made up of the Dog, Tiger and Horse and of these three animal signs, it is the Horse who occupies a cardinal direction (South). The Three Killings is thus in the North, the direction that is directly opposite the Horse.

This affliction causes situations to arise that bring loss of one's good reputation, loss of a loved one and loss of wealth. It is the most common cause of reversals of fortune. In 2018, it occupies the North, so the danger here is to the middle son of the family. Anyone occupying the North likewise suffers this affliction.

Place the right kind of cures to effectively dissolve the energy chi of the Three Killings. Doing this is sure to help you avoid whatever nasty consequences may arise. The Three Killings derail the best laid plans with unexpected obstacles that slow you down and even cause you defeat.

In terms of cures, we have been using the **Three Celestial Protectors** – comprising the Chi Lin, Fu Dog and Pi Yao with great success for several years now. In 2018, you can continue to use these celestials crafted in red colour.

Lined up together, these celestials create a sufficiently powerful and invisible shield of protective energy that prevents the Three Killings from passing into the home or office. In 2018, it is a good idea to keep all North sector doors and windows closed during the afternoon hours, as this will help block the Three Killings energy.

DO NOT RENOVATE NORTH IN 2018!
It is imperative that everyone observes the NO RENOVATION rule for the North this year. Any kind of demolition or digging work here is dangerous in 2018, as this causes negative luck to manifest.

It is especially dangerous to drill floors, knock down walls, dig holes in the ground, engage in any kind of destructive work or make too much noise. These activities activate the Five Yellow which triggers severe misfortune luck to come the way of the household. Protect against this happening. Keep the North quiet.

If you must undertake renovations in your house and it encroaches into the North sector, make sure your cures are prominently in place AND make very sure the renovation does not start or end in the North. No one should be staying in the North sector, when renovations are going on.

BUT: Those building something here in the North, i.e. adding to it, please note that this can be auspicious, since adding to the space is not the same as disturbing the space. Even then, it is better not to take the risk, as you may have to demolish something or dig the earth/floor before you can add to the space. It is advisable to postpone whatever you may be planning for the sector until the following year.

1 Place the mantra enhanced **Five Element Pagoda** at the front of the house.

2 Place the **Eight Hums Protection Wheel** inside the house at the foyer area.

THINGS TO DO IN 2018 IF YOU LIVE IN A NORTH-FACING HOUSE OR A NORTH-LOCATED ROOM

3 Keep the front lights of the house turned off or dimmed through the year.

4 Keep the front of the door quiet and use another door if possible.

5 Place salt inside a brass container to suppress any ongoing bad luck.

APPEASING TAI SUI IN THE NORTHWEST

The Tai Sui is the "God of the Year" which changes location each year. The 2018, Tai Sui has moved to the Northwest into the location of the Dog. Those having their bedroom in this part of the home must not however sit facing the Tai Sui (i.e. NW1) and instead have the Tai Sui supporting you.

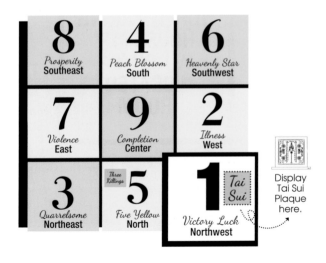

8 *Prosperity* **Southeast**	4 *Peach Blossom* **South**	6 *Heavenly Star* **Southwest**
7 *Violence* **East**	9 *Completion* **Center**	2 *Illness* **West**
3 *Quarrelsome* **Northeast**	*Three Killings* 5 *Five Yellow* **North**	1 Tai Sui *Victory Luck* **Northwest**

Display Tai Sui Plaque here.

THE FENG SHUI OF THE TAI SUI

This is something everyone should take seriously. It is stressed in the famous Treatise on Harmonizing Times and Distinguishing Directions compiled under the patronage of the Qianlong Emperor during his reign in the mid-Eighteenth century. The Emperor placed great credence on astrology and feng shui, and had made a decree that all disagreements regarding the correct ways for selecting times and aligning houses should be reconciled and should then be properly assembled and catalogued for posterity.

The Treatise confirms that the concept of the Tai Sui has been recognized since mid-century BCE (for over 2000 years) and it states that the locations where the Tai Sui resides and where the Tai Sui has just vacated are lucky locations.

This implies it is lucky to be in the Northwest 1 location of the house (where the Tai Sui resides in 2018) and also to be in the West 2 location where the Tai Sui has just vacated. Indeed, experts who have observed the feng shui of the Tai Sui for many years agree that in 2018 the Dog who resides where the Tai Sui resides benefits from the support of the Tai Sui. And anyone who has a room or office in the Northwest 1 location will likewise benefit.

The Treatise explains that it is unlucky to reside in the location where the Tai Sui is progressing towards i.e. clockwise on the astrology compass; and it is also unlucky when one directly confronts the Tai Sui's residence. It is unlucky to "face" the Tai Sui because this is confrontational, so the advice for 2018 is to refrain from facing Northwest 1. This is an inauspicious direction, even if it is personally lucky for those who belong to the West group of directions under the Kua formula.

Confronting the Grand Duke always brings misfortune, failure and loss. When you face the Tai Sui, nothing you do will go smoothly. Obstacles surface unexpectedly and friends turn into adversaries. Thus the Dog should not face its own home direction in 2018 and instead should have its back protected by the Tai Sui. This means facing Southeast 1. Everyone else - all other animal signs - should follow this same advice.

It is very beneficial to place the beautiful **Pi Yao** in the Northwest, as this celestial chimera is incredibly auspicious. For getting on the good side of the Tai Sui, they are also effective. They bring exceptional good fortune into the home. It is also beneficial to Carry the **Tai Sui Amulet of 2018** to get his support.

Place the Pi Yao in the NW1 sector of your home to appease the Tai Sui this year and to get him onto your side. You can also carry the Tai Sui Amulet.

#7 VIOLENT STAR
IN THE EAST

In 2018, the star that brings the bad luck of robbery and violence flies to the East, which is the place of the eldest son and the home location of those born in the year of the Rabbit. This affliction does not bode well for the sector and all who reside here, as it brings the danger of violence and burglary.

If possible, do avoid working or living in this sector, and if your bedroom or front door is located in the East, put the cure against this

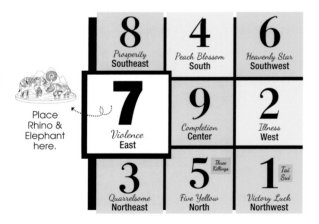

Place Rhino & Elephant here.

8 Prosperity Southeast	4 Peach Blossom South	6 Heavenly Star Southwest
7 Violence East	9 Completion Center	2 Illness West
3 Quarrelsome Northeast	5 Three Killings Five Yellow North	1 Tai Sui Victory Luck Northwest

affliction. The **Blue Rhino and Elephant** drawn with the water motif and with the protective mantra have proved to be very workable as a preventive against robbery.

This affliction is brought by the number 7. This number brings political turmoil and sparks aggressive behavior that lead to serious loss. It brings out the worst in all who come under its influence or is afflicted by it, and in 2018 it is an even more dangerous star. This is because 7 is Metal and it is lethal in the East. In the cycle of the Elements, Metal destroys Wood!

The best cure for the #7 star which brings robbery and violence are the Blue Rhino and Elephant with water motif.

Note also that in the year 2018, the luck stars of the 24 Mountains for the East bring not one but TWO stars that cause problems - these are the stars of the *Yearly Conflict* and the *Yin House*. This indicates that robbery can end in severe tragedy. But in East 3 there is a *Star of Big Auspicious,* which brings something very lucky to those whose room are in this part of the East sector i.e. East 3. This is thus the solution – move your chair or bed to this part of the East sector, and activate here the manifestation of the *Star of Big Auspicious.*

The best way to overcome the negative effect of #7 is to have a **water feature** as water exhausts the vitality of 7. Water is also auspicious for the East, where it strengthens the intrinsic Wood energy here.

Those who already have a water feature here such as a pond in the garden or an internal water feature in the living room will be happy to know that in addition to generating good fortune luck for the eldest son of the family, water also suppresses the burglary star.

So in 2018, water in the East creates a powerful shield against getting robbed and cheated. Those who have a door situated in the East might want to consider creating some kind of water feature here. Another powerful protective shield against getting burgled are of course Rhinos and Elephants. For 2018, the Blue Rhino (and also water features decorated with the Blue Rhino) continue to be effective. Elephants with trunks up are excellent.

However, for added effect and to bring prosperity, it is a good idea to generate the **power of 9**. In 2018, the year of the Dog, displaying "Nine Dogs" sounds very auspicious and also brings incredible good fortune.

You can activate the incredible Power of 9 in 2018 by displaying celestial creatures in sets of 9.

1 Display a **Rhino (double horned)** flanking your front door on the outside.

2 Place a water feature just inside or outside the main door.

THINGS TO DO IN 2018 IF YOU LIVE IN A **EAST-FACING HOUSE** OR A **EAST-LOCATED ROOM**

3 Place nine Elephants/ Rhinos here for added prosperity.

4 Paint your front wall blue to simulate Water chi energy.

5 Display the "Nine Dogs" here.

#8 HIGH AUSPICIOUS STAR IN SOUTHEAST SHOULD BE ACTIVATED

According to the Pa Kua 8 Aspirations method, the Southeast location is the **Asset Wealth** sector of any building. The Trigram SUN that rules the Southeast is associated with the wind that brings prosperity. This symbolizes the successful accumulation of assets over time, assets brought by the winds. When water is placed in the SE, it combines with wind to bring the wealth of wind and water.

$ 8 $ *Prosperity* **Southeast**	4 *Peach Blossom* **South**	6 *Heavenly Star* **Southwest**
7 *Violence* **East**	9 *Completion* **Center**	2 *Illness* **West**
3 *Quarrelsome* **Northeast**	5 Three Killings *Five Yellow* **North**	1 Tai Sui *Victory Luck* **Northwest**

In 2018, the Southeast location is identified as the luckiest sector in any home because it enjoys the auspicious #8 star. This symbolizes the strong energy of the current period, and being one of three white numbers, it is intrinsically lucky.

Meanwhile, #8 is one of the three Earth Element numbers (the others being 2 and 5). As 2018 is a Double Earth year, #8 is in sync with the year energy. These attributes strengthen the significance of #8 in 2018 tremendously. It makes the Southeast a special place, which can be honoured to activate the auspicious energies of the #8.

We strongly recommend placing **Zangdok Palyri** the magical Copper Mountain Home of Guru Rinpoche here, to create the vibrations of a celestial abode in this sector of your home. We have made a fitting likeness of this celestial mansion, and filling it with wish-granting and multiplying mantras makes it a powerfully enhancing presence in the home.

If your bedroom is located in this part of the house and you invite this celestial mansion into your home, it will benefit you tremendously. Likewise, all other members of the household also benefit.

There is also a *Star of Big Auspicious* that sits between the Dragon and Rabbit locations, so you can also place the celestial mansion in exactly E3 location of the home to manifest something big coming to you. In the SE3 sector, the luck star here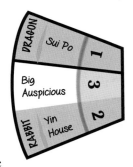

is the *Heavenly Seal Star* which brings "Heaven's Authority". Those residing in this sector can look forward to a year of good fortune.

This star can be activated when there is a *hei see* such as a marriage, a birth or a special elderly person's birthday celebration. The happiness occasion is powerful for bringing pure yang energy to activate the Heaven Seal.

To maximize the luck of #8, it should be thoroughly imbued with yang energy wherever it appears. This means **activity, noise and bright lights.** When there is movement, sound and laughter, the #8 comes to life, bringing good fortune and yards of prosperity.

In the constellation, 8 is a "man-made star" with two assistants – on the right and left. When it is strong, it brings wealth and great nobility.

1. Invite in the celestial mansion of **Guru Rinpoche** into your home.

THINGS TO DO IN 2018 IF YOU LIVE IN A **SOUTHEAST-FACING / SITTING HOUSE**

2. Place lucky **windchimes** here to activate the #8 lucky star.

3. Hosting parties this year attracts in lucky yang energy.

4. Or keep this sector well lit. This strengthens the #8 star in the Southeast.

#1 WHITE STAR OF VICTORY IN NORTHWEST

The white star 1 is associated with winning and attaining success over the competition, so it generally brings Victory Luck to those enjoying its good influences. In 2018, it benefits residents whose bedrooms are located in the Northwest, so if yours is in this sector, you will enjoy Victory Luck manifesting for you.

The number 1 star is a white number, which brings good fortune to those in leadership positions. It benefits the Patriarch who also

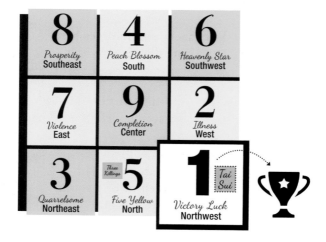

benefits from the positive luck stars of the 24 Mountains that occupy the NW1 (the *Tai Sui* or God of the Year) and the NW2 location (*Star of Small Auspicious*).

It is definitely advantageous to the Patriarch (irrespective of animal sign) when you activate the Northwest, especially when this corresponds to the front part of the house. The best enhancers to place here are **symbols of wealth and prosperity** such as treasure chests, golden ingots and metallic windchimes with auspicious hangings.

Here, the presence of auspicious objects such as images made of precious stones such as jade or crystals would also be very beneficial. Those engaged in competitive sports or endeavours can activate Victory Luck by displaying the **Banner of Victory in the NW**.

The benefits of the **Metal Element** in the Northwest will also be excellent, as this element will strengthen and wake up its super yang essence. Thus **windchimes** would be excellent placed here.

1 Place a carved celestial creature such as a **Pi Yao** or a **Fu Dog** made of precious stone in the foyer or living room facing the door.

THINGS TO DO IN 2018 IF YOU LIVE IN A NORTHWEST-FACING / SITTING HOUSE

2 Place metallic auspicious **windchimes** at the your front door of your house.

3 Paint a rock (or a pile of rocks) golden and place in Northwest.

#6 HEAVENLY STAR IN THE SOUTHWEST

The luck of the powerful Southwest sector, the place of the Matriarch is energized in 2018 with the number 6, which is the star that brings the luck of heaven. This number brings the promise of celestial guidance and assistance, so residents occupying this part of the house will enjoy luck that is unexpected and represent something of a windfall.

This number has been interpreted as bringing gambling and speculative luck. The number 6 is a

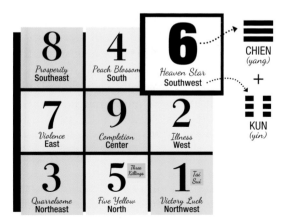

123

white star associated with the powerful Trigram CHIEN, so its presence in the Southwest where the trigram is Kun forms a perfect formation of ultimate yang with ultimate yin.

In this sector, the Matriarch welcomes the Patriarch in a symbolic pairing that is most auspicious for married couples. The 6 suggests heaven's blessings. What strengthens the number is the presence of the *Star of Golden Deity*, which gives added weight to the idea of receiving celestial blessings. In SW1, the luck star is the *Star of Yi Duo*, which suggests that residents in this part of the house or office can do well in 2018 without having to put in much effort.

The *Star of Yi Duo* benefits those born in the year of the Sheep.

This star brings a "multiplying" effect to extreme good fortune, or extreme misfortune when paired with an unlucky star. It is that kind of luck star that can bring either very good or very bad luck to the sector. In 2018, this star in the SW is paired with the number 6, so it brings extreme good fortune. The *Yi Duo Star* this year is thus extremely beneficial for the Sheep sign.

> In 2018, the luck of residents living the Southwest are sure to benefit from **Heaven's blessings,** and such households enjoy a smooth year with few obstacles.

In the current Period of 8, the Southwest is the place to activate for wealth luck, as this is the *Indirect Spirit* of the Period. Having a **water feature** here is beneficial. If you supplement this with bright lights, it will strengthen the Earth Element, bringing great good fortune to the Matriarch, which emanates to the rest of the family.

1 Make sure you have a water feature to activate Indirect Spirit in the Southwest.

2 Place **6 bright lights** here to strengthen Matriarchal energy.

THINGS TO DO IN 2018 IF YOU LIVE IN A SOUTHWEST-FACING HOUSE OR A SOUTHWEST-LOCATED ROOM

3 **Water feature** in Southwest also very auspicious.

4 Display **Wealth God** in Southwest to activate Star of Golden Deity.

CHAPTER 5

LOVE LUCK OF SHEEP 2018

New love opportunities set your heart alight!

COMPATIBILITY WITH EACH ANIMAL SIGN IN 2018

COMPATIBILITY	LUCK OUTLOOK IN 2018
SHEEP & RAT	Not an easy match
SHEEP & OX	Astrological adversaries battle through the year
SHEEP & TIGER	An amiable but unexciting relationship
SHEEP & RABBIT	Immediate affinity for these astrological allies
SHEEP & DRAGON	Happiness for this vibrant couple
SHEEP & SNAKE	Mutual admiration makes for a delightful couple
SHEEP & HORSE	Secret friends and soulmates forever
SHEEP & SHEEP	Synergistic on the surface but may not last
SHEEP & MONKEY	More a partnership than a marriage
SHEEP & ROOSTER	An exhausting pair
SHEEP & DOG	Ho Tu combination helps this pair in 2018
SHEEP & BOAR	Two allies enjoying a good year together

LOVE LUCK OF THE SHEEP IN 2018
New love opportunities set your heart alight!

The Sheep sign is extremely blessed in this Year of the Earth Dog. The *Heaven Star* brings all kinds of opportunities to the Sheep, and for those of you looking for love and romance, something wonderful could be awaiting you just around the corner. The kind of love you can find this year is the sort that creates butterflies in your stomach, that can make your heart sing and set your heart alight.

Do not settle for an ordinary kind of love. There are quite magical things in store for the Sheep, and if you make do with the first option you have, you will miss out on what you truly deserve. The Sheep is one of the most romantic signs. Don't allow yourself to become jaded with life. If you are still single, the love of a lifetime is still out there waiting to be found. With your luck this year, you stand every chance of meeting someone you can truly call your soulmate.

For some of you, there could be a rekindling of an old love affair; sometimes you need time apart but if you are meant for each other, your paths will cross once again. Love works in mysterious ways for the Sheep, and this year it works truly in your favour. The Sheep who's already married will find new things to love about one another, and can embark on new adventures together. It is a honeymoon kind of year, and it does not matter if you are newly acquainted, just married, or a long-time couple happily growing old together.

Enjoy what the year has in store for you!

THE DREAMY FEMALE SHEEP

The lady of the Sheep sign is a gentle soul who is always willing to please, but she is great fun as well. Her sense of humour is fantastic and you often find her the life and soul of the party. While socially she is a big hit, she is a homebody at heart who loves nothing more than to cosy up to her love partner by a warm fire or indoors with a good book.

As a love partner, she is supportive and loyal, but is happy to let her partner lead, decide and take responsibility. However, that does not mean she meekly follows; far from it. She wields her influence in the most subtle of ways, and will always have it appear that her man is making all the decisions. Hers is an understated demeanour, where she would rather play the femme fatale than the dominatrix.

Sheep ladies are rarely madly ambitious for a corporate career, and prefer to support their husbands as hardworking wives. She makes the ultimate trophy wife because her social skills are second to none, and as a mother, she is fiercely protective and watchful over her brood. Cross her and you will feel the wrath of her horns. She is no walkover, although outwardly, she will always display a mild and tender manner.

With a Sheep lady, there will rarely be open conflict or confrontations. She is the ultimate diplomat and will never openly reveal her inner feelings. She makes a dangerous enemy because you cannot even tell if you have offended or wronged her. She will confound even her worst adversaries with niceties.

Famous Sheep ladies include Julia Roberts, Kate Hudson, Bo Derek, Rosamunde Pike, Rose Byrne and Zhang Zi Yi.

THE ROMANTIC MALE SHEEP

The male of the Sheep sign is cunning, manipulative and unpredictable. He is probably the Chinese zodiac's most insidious politician. He always plays his game with his cards close to his chest, cultivating an image of dignified morality. He often comes across placid, unruffled and vague, but underneath the tranquil exterior, he will be hatching one great scheme after another.

The male Sheep is extremely ambitious, and he thinks very big indeed. His aspirations often include power, wealth and influence, but he never reveals his ambitions openly. In business, he will build layers of protective structures that shield him from having to deal with anyone he would rather avoid. He stalks his competition covertly and carefully. In politics, he can be ruthless and devoid of scruples.

The male Sheep usually has few friends, but those he considers close to him, he treats as family. In love, he is adventurous, imaginative and wildly romantic. He will thrill whoever he is romancing with all the trimmings, and will annihilate any competition with his perseverance and his intellect. To be with the Sheep gentleman, you will need to be prepared to bow to his wishes. He will seek out partners who can dream big with him. While he appreciates outward beauty, what is even more important to him is that he can connect beyond a physical level.

He does not take well to being challenged, and unlike his female counterpart, the male Sheep will not shy away from a fight. And he will fight openly. He is a master at his game and approaches any challenge like a game of chess. Unless his rivals put in as mcuh strategic effort as him, he will win out every time.

Sheep men make good patriarchs in that they will provide well for their family, but he may not be an always present parent. He is too ambitious and his work often takes him away from home. If you want to hook a Sheep gentleman, you will need to be the one to compromise, because he will not. But when he is in love, he makes all his idosynchracies worth putting up with.

Famous Sheep gentlemen include Bill Gates, Steve Jobs, Bruce Willis, Chris Pratt, James McAvoy.

ACTIVATING FOR LOVE & MARRIAGE

The single Sheep who has not yet found someone of interest can do so by activating their Peach Blossom luck. Your Peach Blossom Animal is the **Rat**. It is said that within three months you will be able to find love, the kind of love that has a good chance of leading to marriage. This method will also work for those of you who have been going steady but with one partner unwilling to commit or set the date.

> Display a grand-looking **Rat** in the North sector of your bedroom to activate for love, and better if you can light up your Peach Blossom animal.

For the Sheep-born this year, the best month to find love is September - this is when the romance star enters your chart - so in September, if you are single and looking for love, stay extra aware of the people entering your life. The "one" could be among them. And when you spot them, make an effort to woo them or to make your feelings known. The Sheep is enjoying a really wonderful year when it comes to love, so if you are serious about finding someone you can share a life-long rmance with, it is worth making the effort this year.

In 2018, everyone else can also activate love luck in general by displaying a Horse in the South. The South is where the *#4 Romance Star* of the year has flown into, and activating this sector will benefit all animal signs.

A Horse in the South will also make other relationships more amiable, so if you have been finding it more of a challenge to maintain harmony on the relationship front, get a Horse figurine and display in the South part of the home. You can also display horses in the form of art, by hanging a beautiful painting.

MAINTAINING A HAPPY MARRIAGE

This year's chart features the *External Flower of Romance Star,* which affects everyone irrespective of your animal sign. If you have been married a long time and your interests have diverged over the years, it is easy to have less and less in common. And if temptation comes along for either of you from an outside source, the *External Flower of Romance* this year could cause one of you to stray.

If you feel you are in danger of losing your husband or wife to someone else, wear or carry the **Marriage Saver Medallion.** This will help keep your marriage strong and prevent both sides from succumbing to temptation.

Try to find common ground again, perhaps a new activity, sport or hobby. Or make the effort to arrange a holiday together. It is important to spend time together away from the stresses of everyday life to remind yourselves of the love you share, so do make the effort here.

COMPATIBILITY WITH POTENTIAL PARTNERS

The Chinese believe that when there is Zodiac compatibility between two people, chances of a union succeeding is greatly enahnced. That is why in the old days, Chinese families would never arrange marriages for their sons and daughters without first checking compatibility on various fronts. Of course, in today's world, most marriages are no longer arranged and are left to fate and chance. But having some natural affinity with your partner will make things a lot smoother, with a love that can endure with minimal effort. Here are several ways you can check compatibility with a potential mate:

Horoscope Allies & Affinity Triangles

Your horoscope allies are the other two animal signs that make up an affinity triangle in the astrological chart. The Sheep belongs to the triangle of affinity made up of the **Sheep**, the **Rabbit** and the **Boar.** This means that for the Sheep, should you get together with someone born under the sign of Rabbit or Boar, you are sure to get along with each other. You have a natural sensitivity to each others feelings and are

The Sheep, Rabbit and Boar belong to the Astrological Ally Grouping of Diplomats.

more understanding of each other's insecurities. There is fabulous potential to build a happy marriage and family life together. This kind of affinity also applies to your children, so a new Sheep parent planning to start or enlarge your family can choose ally years to have children.

If you all belong to the same affinity triangle, chances of continuous family harmony are considerably enhanced. Your affinity traingle make up the "Diplomats" of the Chinese Zodiac. As a group, you are sociable, sympathethic and eager to please. You are not necessarily big risk takers, but you do enjoy the occasional thrill. For you, security especially of the material kind is important. Your similar ways of thinking leads to a more harmonious home and family life if you are married to one of your astrological allies. A long-term relationship between you and either of these signs is likely to be filled with understanding and empathy.

Borrowing good luck from your allies

This year, the Rabbit is the strongest of your affinity triangle of allies, having the best element luck, so the Rabbit can lend strength to the Sheep and Boar. The Rabbit however has the #7 star, which brings danger of loss, particularly money loss. The Sheep meanwhile has the *#6 Heaven Star*, while the Boar has the lucky *#1 Victory Star*.

Displaying the three allied signs of Rabbit, Sheep and Boar in your home sector of Southwest will allow you to tap on the good fortune aspects of your allies. Having a Rabbit or Boar partner - in love or business - will also bring you reflected glory and joint success.

Your Secret Friend, the Horse

The Sheep's secret friend is the Horse. The Sheep and Horse together provide each other with seamless love and support. Being each other's secret friend means it will be difficult for outside parties to come between you. You will always take each other's side first. You are also excellent for each other from a luck perspective; your union brings you the good fortune afforded to secret friend pairings.

The Sheep's secret friend is the Horse. The two of you are wonderful for each other, providing unwavering support and bringing good fortune luck just by being together.

Secret friends

The Sheep and Horse make a wonderful couple in love, but you also do well together in business, as best pals or in a parent-child or mentor-child relationship. You are helpful to each other both overtly and covertly. You are both both highly industrious and courageous, and you operate on the same wavelength.

Your Soulmate, the Horse

In the Chinese Zodiac, there are six pairings whose chemistry is undeniable. When these pairs come together, there is natural empathy and attraction between you. The different pairings conjure up different kinds of luck, but always, the pairing produces a bond that can stand the test of time. These pairings are sometimes known as Soulmate Pairings, and for the Sheep, your astrological soulmate is the Horse.

Together, the Sheep and Horse form the *House of Passion and Sexuality*. This means that when you get together with someone born in the year of the Horse, all kinds of sparks fly! There is incredible sexual chemistry and after that, there is more! You are both physically and mentally attracted to one another, and because you are secret friends as well as soulmates, your relationship is unlike any other zodiac pairing. The Sheep and Horse both see only the most positive qualities in each other and you become each other's greatest support and life companion.

ASTROLOGICAL
SOULMATE PAIRINGS

Tiger & Rabbit
*House of Growth &
Development*

Horse & Sheep
*House of Passion &
Sexuality*

Rat & Ox
*House of Creativity
& Cleverness*

Dog & Boar
House of Domesticity

Rooster & Monkey
*House of Career &
Commerce*

Snake & Dragon
*House of Magic &
Spirituality*

Same KUA group

When you share the same Kua group as your partner, whatever is lucky for one of you is lucky for the other. It is easy then for you to design the feng shui of your home together when you are both East group, or when you are both West group. And when both in a pair are enjoying good fortune, it is easier to be amiable and to get along. Note however that you do NOT have to be in the same group Kua group to be compatible. It simply makes life easier from a feng shui viewpoint.

Sum-of-Ten Compatibility

If your Kua numbers add up to a sum of ten, this indicates great potential to be auspicious. I.e. if your Kua number is 1 and your partner's Kua is 9, you form a sum of 10 together. Or if your Kua number is 3 and your partner's is 7, and so on. Note that if you make up the sum-of-ten pairing of 2 and 8, you both belong to the West group but more than that, you represent the Direct and Indirect Spirit of this Period of 8. This makes your pairing even more auspicious, especially during Period of 8. Other sum-of-ten combinations are 4/6, and 5/5.

Ho Tu Compatibility

If your individual Kua numbers form a Ho Tu pairing, there is indication that as a pair, you generate some wonderfully lucky good fortune dimensions. What this means is you bring good luck to one another, and your sum is greater than your parts.

Those with **1 and 6** Ho Tu are very clever people who excel professionally in the arts and sciences. The two of you enjoy a meaningful and fulfilling life together, as you have great intellectual compatibility.

Those with **2 and 7** Ho Tu can generate great wealth together, as there is *Big Money Luck* in this combination.

Those with **3 and 8** Ho Tu will have great social authority and influence as a couple. You have a future as natural leaders or as influential trendsetters. This pairing indicates a life of power and authority.

The **4 and 9** Ho Tu pairing enjoy excellent business luck together. If you two start a commercial venture together, you are sure to do very well indeed.

Paht Chee Affinity

Even if you and your partner do not fall into one of the previously mentioned natural compatibility groupings, you could be well-matched based if you have each other's Chinese Zodiac signs in your respective *Paht Chee* charts.

When your animal sign is present in your partner's Paht Chee chart, and especially when it appears in the **Month Pillar**, it means your relationship contains karmic links to each other. It is very auspicious and whoever has the other's animal sign in the **Day Pillar** will hold the power in the relationship. If your sign is in your partner's **Hour Pillar,** it means you are compatible and happy to be in the subordinate role in the relationship.

Your Incompatible Animal Sign

Here is a pairing that is not so beneficial for you; this is when you and your partner are zodiac adversaries. The Sheep's incompatible animal sign is the **Ox**. This is the animal sign located directly opposite you in the Zodiac wheel. If this is the scenario you have, then it is better not to take things any further. Long term prospects for this union are not so promising; and chances of splitting up are high. Even if passion flows between you at the early stages of your relationship, you are not likely to stay together in the long term.

The Sheep and Ox are better off pairing up with other signs who have more to offer in the compatibility stakes. But if you are already together as a couple and would like things to work out, display a Rat (the secret friend of the Ox) in your own sector of Southwest).

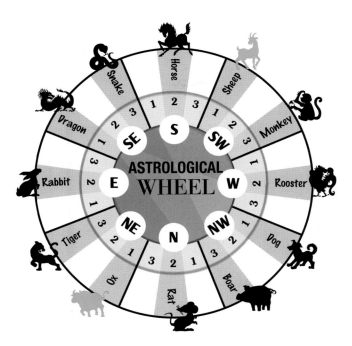

The animal sign directly opposite you in the Zodiac does not have so much affinity with you. It is better not to pair up with your incompatible animal sign if you want your union to be harmonious. But if you are already in a relationship, the solution is to display the secret friend of the Ox, which is the Rat, in your home sector of Southwest. The rat is also your Peach Blossom Animal, which brings double the benefit.

COMPATIBILITIES IN 2018

Compatibility between different animal signs will differ from year to year, and change as the energies affecting each sign changes. When one sign is weaker relative to others, it will do much better when paired up with signs who have stronger charts. This way they can go some way to "borrowing" the luck of their partner. Put two animal signs who are going through bad years together and you are just asking for disaster.

The following pages indicate compatibility between the **SHEEP** and the other Chinese Zodiac signs. Note that here we are talking about compatibility in 2018, the Year of the Earth Dog. The long-standing compatibilities talked about previously in this chapter hold more weight and should be given priority when picking a partner.

This section of the book will however help you navigate things if you are already with someone, or it can give you a heads up on who to go with if there is more than one potential suitor on the horizon. We also indicate pairings that have potential not just in love, but in friendships and business where it applies.

SHEEP & RAT

Not an easy match

While the Rat is the Sheep's *Peach Blossom Animal*, you are both signs that need constant reassurance. Because you are both quite needy for encouragement, it will be difficult for either of you to provide adequate amounts of this for each other. Unless you work at getting a mutual admiration society going between you, both will feel an easing off of passions after the initial dating period is over.

> These are two signs that can enjoy the good times together, but weathering bad times may get too difficult, even impossible.

The Rat can appear very loud to the soft-spoken Sheep, while the Sheep's gentle demeanour could grate on Rat's nerves. The Rat's solution to any problem is one full of bravado, while the Sheep prefers to simply trot away from a problem. Dealing with real life problems will soon see this relationship hit potholes that could damage egos and self-esteem. When things get tough, it will be difficult for either Sheep or Rat to be the strong one. Both would rather be with a partner who can give them the encouragement and strength they need, even if only behind closed doors. Neither of you need any of your battles fought for you, but you certainly would like your partner to offer.

In 2018, the Sheep is enjoying much better luck than the poor Rat. When Rat needs a strong shoulder to lean on, the Sheep is unlikely to provide. Meanwhile, the Sheep is probably busy pursuing its own lofty goals, and the Rat will find it difficult to keep cheering the Sheep on, even as it is going through such a difficult year itself.

There are serious difference in attitudes, which could cause major disagreements to occur. While Rat is not one to hold a grudge, Sheep however will not let things go so easily. Sheep has a tendency to take things to heart, and when it feels hurt or aggrieved, it will not forgive so easily. Rat meanwhile has the propensity to keep saying the wrong things and making the wrong moves in the eye of the Sheep. If something has only just started, take things slow. It may not be such a good idea to rush into a Sheep/Rat union; and chances of it lasting into the long term are slim.

SHEEP & OX

Astrological adversaries battle through the year

The Sheep and Ox are natural enemies in the astrological wheel, so it will be difficult to make this pairing work unless there are other factors working to keep you two together. But you are both Earth signs, and your similar elements could spark some initial attraction.

Early days between a Sheep and an Ox can be full of passion and ardour. But when the flames settle, you may find little left over to form a proper backbone for the relationship.

In 2018, the Ox is troubled by the *Quarrelsome Star*, while the Sheep enjoys the *#6 Heaven Star*. In terms of disposition, Sheep will tend to be in a much more amiable mood than the Ox, and will have to be the one to constantly give in. If the Sheep has reason enough to make things work, it can bend backwards and be the one to give in. But this will only happen if the Sheep wants it enough. The Ox is a no-nonsense kind of person, while the Sheep is much more emotional. The two of you possess entirely different vibes, and while you can banter quite happily in public, when you two are alone, there is too little in common to make this relationship work long-term.

While you are both ambitious types, you have hugely differing priorities in life, as well as completely different ways of approaching things. Your individual strengths are poles apart, and while two people with different fortes can usually find a better fit, bringing different skills to the table, with Sheep and Ox, this is sadly not the case.

You do not see eye-to-eye and this often leads to frustration and anger. Ox likes to think things through and decide based on careful deliberation. Sheep likes to consult with anyone and everyone. Ox will often consider the Sheep's friendliness an invasion of privacy into their union, while the Sheep will find it difficult to have just the Ox for counsel or company.

It will be difficult to make this pairing work, whether in love or in business. As friends, there is a certain camaraderie, but get too close and even that harmony quickly breaks down.

SHEEP & TIGER

An amiable but unexciting relationship

The Sheep and Tiger have precious little in common, but sometimes opposites can attract. In this case, Sheep and Tiger can sometimes find each other suitable spouse material, although deep and abiding passion will be somewhat missing. When Sheep and Tiger get together, there will be very little communication.

What passes between Sheep and Tiger lacks conviction and they can even be described as a fair weather couple, enduring each other only so long as there is mutual advantage. When this evaporates, so too will the relationship.

But if the Sheep and Tiger have shared goals and aspirations, there is a future for this pair together. In the eyes of the extrovert Tiger, the Sheep comes across meek, subtle and unexciting. Until of course Tiger goes deeper and finds there is more behind Sheep's quiet demeanour. When they do find each other is when both sides are actively "looking" for a special something. Effort is needed for this pair to take off as an "item" because initially, there is little natural attraction.Usually it is when the Tiger is a little older before he/she is able to appreciate someone as subtle as the Sheep. At a younger age, the wiles and wisdom of the Sheep can go completely over the head of the Tiger, who tends to appreciate the obvious more than the subtle. The Sheep meanwhile rarely if ever feels comfortable living the kind of lifestyle that the young Tiger likes. This couple rarely takes a confrontational stand against one another. Sheep makes sure of that, so a semblance of politeness will always prevail.

In 2018, when the Sheep enjoys the *Star of Heaven*, Tiger will find Sheep extremely attractive, but Sheep is likely to have many admirers, and chances of Sheep responding to Tiger's overtures are slim... unless Tiger tries real hard. As for the Tiger, if love and attraction is not immediately reciprocated, he/she will not bend backwards very far to make things work.

This is a match frowned upon by most Chinese grandmothers, because according to superstition, a match between a Tiger and a small animal will result in the small animal being "eaten up".

SHEEP & RABBIT

Immediate affinity for these astrological allies

The Sheep and Rabbit make a simply wonderful couple. These are two beautifully matched individuals who have little trouble striking up immediate affinity with one another. The usually secretive Sheep opens up to the astute and diplomatic Rabbit, while the Rabbit responds to the delightfully seductive Sheep.

Sheep and Rabbit belong to the affinity triangle of Diplomats and both have very similar styles and approaches to living. Neither are risk takers and both prefer a quiet, stable lifestyle, although each provides exactly the kind of encouragement the other needs.

Both are quietly ambitious but will rarely admit to it, preferring to let their results speak for themselves. They will seldom reveal their hopes or aspirations, but with each other, they are much happier to open up. Rabbit fuels Sheep's confidence, while Sheep provides a good sounding board for Rabbit's notions and ideas, no matter how idealistic or impracticle they may be.

Together, Rabbit and Sheep can build a beautiful life and a nurturing home together.

In this pairing, it will usually be the Rabbit who will skilfully draw out all of the Sheep's latent and hidden talents, while the Sheep thrives with the love and attention of the doting Rabbit. They are genuinely happy for one another when each succeeds, so in this union, there is no competitive element to drive a wedge between them.

This is a pairing that enjoys both physical attraction as well as a meeting of the minds.

The Sheep tends to be the moodier character, but the Rabbit easily soothes the Sheep. The Rabbit meanwhile has clearcut social ambitions, which the Sheep goes a long way to hepl fulfill. Both are highly sociable and popular personalities, so you are likely to find a Sheep-Rabbit couple at all the hottest parties and events around town.

In business, Sheep and Rabbit make a productive pair. There are rarely big disagreements when you work together because you think along the same lines and in the same way.

SHEEP & DRAGON

Happiness for this vibrant couple

This is a pairing between two Earth individuals that bring out the best in each other. The yang Dragon is vibrant and domineering, while the seductive Sheep is docile and yielding. Together, these two make a dreamy couple. There is no fight or tussle for control, because the Dragon clearly leads and the Sheep is all too happy to submit.

The Dragon's obvious charisma appeals to the elegant Sheep, while the Sheep's grace and polish brings out the protective nature in the Dragon.

Between you there is always excellent communication and each can match the other in both intellect and talent. While your approches to life and living can be quite different, your diverse strengths compliment each other nicely.

There will rarely be heated arguments between you, so yours will be a harmonious union free of temper tantrums or big misunderstandings. The confident Dragon motivates the Sheep, while the composed Sheep calms the headstrong Dragon. You can build a loving family life together, and as a pair of parents, you balance your good cop-bad-cop roles to perfection.

In 2018, there is plenty of success and happiness for this pair. The Dragon enjoys the Wealth Star 8, while the Sheep brings Heaven Luck via the #6. If you team up, there is little you cannot conquer.

In love, there is always natural chemistry between you, and if you have only just met, the year holds out the promise of things developing very quickly between you. Neither will have too much of a problem committing to one another, as long as one of you takes the lead.

While Sheep and Dragon make a divine romantic couple, this pairing also works between a pair of business partners or best friends. The Dragon's blazing nature sets off the Sheep's serene disposition nicely. The Dragon lends the Sheep fire, while the Sheep tempers the Dragon's impetuousness.

SHEEP & SNAKE

Mutual admiration makes for a delightful couple

The Sheep and Snake share more in common than may at first be obvious. On the surface, you come across quite different. The Sheep is sentimental and compassionate, while the Snake appears detached and apathetic. The Sheep tends to get involved in the problems of others, while the Snake rarely has the time or the inclination. But what you do share is the same genuinely compassionate nature, so in the end you usually want the same things.

Snake is taken by Sheep's tender nature, while Sheep admires the Snake's rational approach. In conversation, you can talk for hours on end and not tire of each other. There is most definitely soulmate material in the making if a Snake gets together with a Sheep.

While there are no obvious astrological links, personality-wise, the two of you are extremely compatible. In 2018, a pairing between a Sheep and a Snake is more likely to work than ever, with both of you enjoying very lucky flying stars in your respective sectors. The Snake has the *#8 Prosperity Star*, while the Sheep comes under the blessings of the *Heaven Star #6*.

Individually, you are both going through good years, so emotionally you are both in a good place. Neither are needy, and despite leaning on each other, this will be for affection rather than support.

> Sheep and Snake are two self-sufficient individuals that value each other for all the right reasons. While you can both come across superficial to other signs who may not understand you so well, with each other, you see through to each other's genuine natures.

You are both extremely ambitious, but you usually keep your ambitions concealed. You are do-ers rather than talkers, but with each other, you become more willing to share your innermost thoughts in open discussion. This is an important aspect of the Sheep-Snake pairing, the ability to open up to one another without apprehension or anxiety. A mutually supportive union.

SHEEP & HORSE

Secret friends and soulmates forever

The Sheep and Horse make the most incredible pair. Not only are you secret friends of the Zodiac, you are also soulmates. You form the *House of Passion and Sexuality* with one another. Yours will be a highly physical and extremely passionate relationship. Your union is likely to be characterised by many heated arguments and temper tantrums, but you always make up and become stronger after each altercation.

In 2018, the Horse enjoys the #4 Peach Blossom Star, and this only serves to heighten Sheep's infatuation with the Horse. The Sheep meanwhile is doing extremely well, with the benefit of the *Heaven Star* on its side. And this is not all. Together, your numbers this year form a *sum-of-ten,* so not only do you have tons of fun together, your parts create more than a whole.

What this means is that in 2018 especially, when the Sheep gets together with a Horse, magical things can happen. You make a fabulously popular couple, and if you are working together, your energies jive extremely well allowing your productivity to go sky high. This pairing works no matter what relationship you are in - as lovers, business partners, best friends or work colleagues. You do not suffer from any jealous feelings towards the other, no matter much better one is doing than the other.

Yours is a truly supportive and nurturing kind of pairing, and the nice thing is you take turns looking after each other, so neither one of you will feel you are being taken for granted.

A young Sheep and Horse will have more explosive moments with each other, but as you mature, your highly strung personalities are tamed and the flavour of your relationship transforms from one of exciting but bordering on reckless, to building a secure and happy life together.

Sheep and Horse age extremely well together. Yours is a pairing that will stand the test of time through good times and bad. You make a wonderful couple, and as parents, you divide up your responsibilities superbly, allowing each of you to impart the best of you into your children.

SHEEP & SHEEP

Synergistic on the surface but may not last

Two Sheep together can get along well because you are both so similar. You think along the same lines, you like and dislike the same people, you have the same values, you share common interests. But while two Sheep can make great friends, as a couple, it is a different matter.

Neither of you will take the lead in the relationship, you agree with each other wholeheartedly, the pairing lacks sizzle and spirit. All it will take to shatter your seemingly idealistic existence together is for an outsider to come along. Yours will be a dull pairing where you are neither happy nor unhappy. You co-exist rather than live together, and after a while, you will both crave something more.

The Sheep is not reputedly the most faithful of signs, and temptation can easily cause you to cheat on each other. And when you do, the relationship does not even come to an acrimonious end. Which will prove perhaps the relationship was not ever as solid as it appeared to be.

In 2018, two Sheep can come together as a couple simply because you are both going through good years, and while the Sheep loves beauty, the Sheep is a highly attractive personality itself. There will be physical attraction on first meeting. But for this pairing to stand the test of time could prove more difficult.

Sheep's intrinsic element is Earth, and a double dose of Earth could cause problems when the changing energies feature too much Earth. 2018 is a double Earth year, so problems may well start to surface sooner rather than later.

Two Sheep can get along well and even end up best friends, but you will need to also lead your separate lives and have different friends as an aside from the friends you share. If your lives become too intertwined, it could cause both of you to feel claustrophobic and start searching elsewhere for affection. This pairing however could work if one of you has a strong element in your hour of birth, in which case chances of this union working long term gets significantly enhanced.

SHEEP & MONKEY

More a partnership than a marriage

The Sheep and Monkey can build a beautiful existence together, but while there will be romance to start with, the pairing will only last if your relationship can transcend that onto deeper things. The Monkey is wily and clever, and while the Sheep matches the Monkey in terms of intellect, it is not as worldly-wse as the crafty Monkey. This pairing will always work better when the Monkey is the male in the relationship.

Between Sheep and Monkey, there will always be genuine caring on both sides, and whether you are going through good times or bad, you will be supportive of one another. You are sector mates, so your luck largely moves in unison with one another's, another factor which helps your affinity with one another.

The Sheep's soothing nature is balm to the Monkey's sometimes erratic moods. While the Monkey may sometimes get impatient with the Sheep's meticulous attention to detail, preferring to get things done than perfect, it will come to appreciate the value of Sheep's particular nature. In fact, Sheep and Monkey's strengths compliment each other ver nicely; the Monkey is the big picture person while the Sheep ensures all the specifics are in place. The Monkey paints with a broad stroke, while the Sheep draws with a fine pointed pen.

> You can make beautiful music together as a couple, and your union will be richer and more satisfying if you are not merely lovers but partners in every sense of the word.

In 2018, both Sheep and Monkey enjoy the *Heavenly Star #6,* so both are going through a truly blessed year. Good things happen for both of you, and as a pair, your auspicious energies get doubled.

The Monkey is the *yang* animal in the relationship, while the Sheep is the *yin.* This suggests that the leadership role will be thrust upon the Monkey. Monkey is happy to assume this role, while Sheep is happy to happy to follow. This is a mutually very beneficial pairing, with much love and affection flowing between you.

SHEEP & ROOSTER

An exhausting pair

While Sheep and Rooster can find common ground with each other, there is little natural affinity between you. You get along fine when you do not get too close, but when you do, you tend to start taking each other for granted.

The Rooster takes advantage of Sheep's amiable and easy-going nature to the point when Sheep will rescind its generosity of spirit. The Sheep views Rooster's attempts at humour with suspicion.

It is difficult for Sheep and Rooster to form a genuinely supportive pair, because you often feel in competition with each other. Instead of helping each other, you could end up subconsciously sabotaging one another.

If there is a big age gap between you, this pairing could work better, but if you are only two years apart, the rivalry will always end up coming between you. Yours is a pairing that constantly suffers one-upmanship, one always having to prove him or herself better than the other. You would think you were on different teams!

In 2018, the Sheep has the *#6 Heaven Star,* while the Rooster has the *Illness Star #2.* But Rooster's element luck is far superior to that of the Sheep. The fact your energies are so unbalanced in 2018 however could end up helping the relationship.

It is when you are both similarly strong or similarly weak that troubles will arise for this pairing. When one is obviously lagging the other, the feeling will be one of encouragement rather than rivalry. But when you pull neck to neck will be when feelings of affection turn into feelings of envy and resentment.

In any argument, neither will back down. You are both strong-minded individuals albeit in different ways, but when it comes to a face-off, neither of you will happily give in. Whether your disagreements end in heated tempers or icy stares will depend on your individual personalities, but with time, there will be too many of such incidences for you to want to continue to make this work.

SHEEP & DOG

Ho Tu combination helps this pair in 2018

2018 could see Sheep and Dog come together as a happy, loving and successful couple. Your energies this year blend well, forming the auspicious *1/6 Ho Tu* which brings a matching of minds and a merging of interests. Together you can truly conquer the world, and whether you are lovers, friends or business partners, what you can create as a pair can be quite spectacular in this Year of the Earth Dog.

As personalities, you are both quite different despite you both belonging to the Earth element. The Sheep is as crafty as the Dog is forthright, the Dog loves the limelight while the Sheep is happy to work under the radar. But when you can make your relationship work, you can meet with wonderful combined success.

The Sheep's apparent vulnerability brings out all that is protective of the Dog's instincts. With the Sheep, the Dog is filled with the urge to take care of its Sheep partner. The Sheep meanwhile allows the Dog to take the lead in the union. When you fit into your distinct roles this way, your pairing could work, until Dog tires of Sheep exploiting Dog's compassionate and kind nature. A Sheep-Dog relationship has the danger of becoming very one-sided, with one constantly giving and the other constantly taking. Unless you work at redressing the balance, the initial attraction and chemistry betwene you could eventually fizzle out.

Sheep and Dog work best when both are independently pursuing their own things. It is tempting for Sheep to allow itself to be looked after by the Dog, because Dog appears willing to do so. But if Sheep reliquishes its independence, it will be the first step to demolishing what you have together.

If you are in love and already together, having a baby this year will lift your relationship to new highs. This is because both Dog and Sheep are naturally family people. When Sheep and Dog have something to nurture together, you work extremely well as a team. As parents, you nurture the most talented kids. As business partners, you bring entirely different skills to the table. But when one allows the other to totally dominate, a Sheep-Dog union could start showing holes.

SHEEP & BOAR

Two allies enjoying a good year together in 2018

The Sheep and Boar are astrological allies and make one of the sweetest pairings of the Chinese zodiac in any year. But in 2018 when you both enjoy the lucky white stars of #6 and #1 respectively, your union sees new highs. The Year of the Earth Dog brings windfall luck to the Sheep, and victory energies to the Boar.

In a Sheep and Boar pairing, the sensitive Sheep finds sustenance and love from the Boar, while the Boar takes pride in the Sheep's classy and gentle disposition. You bring each other a lot of joy, but more than that, you can build a very successful and enriching life together.

The Sheep and Boar share the same values and ideals. What is important to one is important to the other, so your goals are always nicely aligned. There are never any severe misunderstandings between, so your household will always be a jovial and good-humoured environment. The Sheep has a wicked sense of humour, which the Boar gets. Both of you enjoy the creature comforts of life, and will happily splurge on something, even if overpriced, if you feel the pleasure you get is worth it. There are no money issues between you, as you are both equally generous.

Sheep and Boar are equally dreamy and romantic, but you are also down-to-earth when it comes to practical matters. You may have your eyes on the stars, but your feet are firmly on the ground.

In love, you enjoy the simple pleasures and neither will be predisposed to succumbing to outside distractions. You have eyes only for each other, and will go the extra mile to help one another out.

The Sheep is of the Earth element, while the Boar is of the Water element. In the cycle of elements, Earth destroys Water. One party is thus clearly in control in this relationship, and in this case it is the Sheep who dominates. But the buckets of natural affinity you share smooths the relationship, and the more aggressive Boar will always give in to the delightful Sheep.

CHAPTER 6

SHEEP'S MONTH BY MONTH LUCK FOR 2018

Heaven luck bestows you with excellent instincts and good judgement

FIRST MONTH
February 4th - March 5th 2018
Energy levels may be low, but you're still on high alert

The Sheep enters the Year of the Dog vaguely lacking in energy, but your spirits are high and you have many grand ideas you would like to set into motion. You cannot embark on everything you want to do by yourself, so you start to rope in others to help. The Sheep's mind is always on overdrive, and as you relinquish control, you wonder if those you entrust with tasks can deliver.

You are quite the perfectionist and your standards are high, but if you are going to stand a chance to achieve all that you envision, doing it alone will not be possible. With this mindset, you begin to build allies for your plan. But rest assured that with the *#6 Heaven Star* on your side, your luck is solid this year, and on the whole, those you work with and place your trust in are largely dependable and upright.

WORK & CAREER - *Teamwork*
This month favours working closely with others. You are feeling mentally agile and energised, but you do not seem to have enough hours in the

day to complete everything you have taken on. When you divide up your tasks, you find your stress levels lifting, and it also becomes a good way to bond more effectively with those you work with. You have no trouble fitting in to a team situation as you are the ultimate diplomat; saying the right things, knowing how much credit to take and how much to give come naturally to you.

Your steadily rising popularity as you come into closer contact with more of your colleagues strengthens you in terms of your future in your firm. The month ahead will be characterised less by competition, and more by collaboration.

BUSINESS - *Managing others*

Effective delegation will see you covering far more ground than you hoped for. This is a stimulating month when you see new opportunities open up for you. There are a number of strategic alliances you can set up, but what may cause you to take pause is wondering whether the people you team up with will be beneficial in the longer term. If you focus on enlarging the pie, there should be little problem keeping everyone satisfied as things progress. You are as astute a business person as ever, and the energies of the year help you make sound decisions. Your appetite for risk increases as you become more ambitious with each success. Those with a large number of employees should focus more attention managing them; even if it takes time out of your own schedule to have more meetings with your staff, the benefits outweigh the effort and will prove more than worthwhile.

LOVE & RELATIONSHIPS - *Faith*
A wonderful time for love! You are feeling romantic and will be happier with a partner than single. Those still looking for the right person may want to look harder. Don't wait to be approached; if there is someone who has caught your eye, make your moves now. The month promises happiness in love, so little can go wrong if you have a little faith.

EDUCATION - *Stretched too thin*
The young Sheep may find yourself being stretched too thin. The *#2 Illness Star* weakens your disposition and gets you tired out more easily. If you have taken on too much, you may start to notice the adverse effects it has on your work. Perhaps reduce the number of extra-curricular activities you commit yourself to.

SECOND MONTH
March 6th - April 4th 2018
Ho Tu brings intellectual luck

You have some fabulous stars in your chart! The *Victory Star #1* flies in to join the resident #6 star, forming the very lucky *1/6 Ho Tu*. This combination brings intellectual luck to the Sheep, giving you improved powers of concentration and boosting your analytical prowess. You raise the bar when it comes to your work, and those involved in highly academic ventures can experience some breakthroughs this month.

The student Sheep will also notice a change; you are feeling more productive and more intelligent. Blocks you may have encountered when your energy levels were down now magically get lifted. The #1 star also brings change of a most beneficial kind. This is a month for new discoveries and personal growth. You end the month a lot wiser than you started it.

FENG SHUI TIP: Display the **1/6 Ho Tu Dragon Carp Stamp** on your workdesk or in your home sector of SW. This is especially beneficial for student Sheep.

WORK & CAREER - *Appreciated*

You are feeling sharp and switched on, and your increased perceptiveness makes you an invaluable member of any team. If last month went well for you, this month promises to be even better. The #1 white star in your chart brings leadership luck, and causes others to naturally look to you for counsel and advice. You act wiser than your years and even those more senior than you acknowledge there are things they can learn from you. Being appreciated by others is a big deal for the Sheep person, and this month, you feel valued.

BUSINESS - *Increasing market share*

The lucky stars in your chart make the Sheep in business even more prolific and industrious. You achieve a lot this month, and with the *#1 Victory Star* in the vicinity, you also enjoy excellent competitive luck. This could be an opportune time to go after more market share, spend on boosting exposure for your brand, or aim at being number one. Dare to dream big; you enjoy the *Big Auspicious* being reflected from across the 24 Mountains Compass this year. This suggests you can achieve success of a mammoth nature.

LOVE - *Feeling independent*
The Sheep is feeling particularly independent and for you to think about settling down with anyone, they will need to be something special. You are not in the kind of mood to fall into someone else's plans. Unless whoever is after you is prepared to put you first, you are unlikely to stay interested. You are looking for commitment and devotion, because the alternative - being single - is also looking quite attractive now.

EDUCATION - *Number One*
A time for the young Sheep to shine! The *Victory Star #1* brings winner's luck into your orbit, giving you an edge over the competition. If you are aiming for the top spot, you have every chance to find it this month.

More exciting is the #1 combining with the #6 to form the *1/6 Ho Tu*, which brings scholastic and intellectual luck. This boosts your powers of concentration and the depth of your understanding in your studies. Activate this luck with the **Dragon Carp Ho Tu Stamp.**

THIRD MONTH
April 5th - May 5th 2018
Magnification Star augments good fortune luck

The pace picks up with the *#9 Fire Star* flying in to fuel the *Heaven Star #6,* as well as the Sheep's intrinsic Earth element. When the #9 star makes an appearance, it usually acts as a multiplier for whatever other stars are making their presence felt. Because you have the *Heaven Star,* this multiplies its benevolent effect, bringing increased opportunities your way. You also benefit from an energy boost, giving you the impetus to pursue leads and make a success of them.

This is a high energy month when you may find yourself with a lot going on, but it will be the good kind of busy. You are not stressed out; rather, you feel invigorated. Your confidence levels are up and you infect others with your enthusiasm. It will be easy for the Sheep to motivate others, and to win them onto your side.

WORK & CAREER - *Exciting times*
The Sheep can make good progress in its career. Mentor luck is strong. If you have the right person backing you, you can go very far in a short

time. Those who are ambitious will benefit the most from the energies of the month, which favour the Sheep who puts in the effort. While it is a time when things "fall into your lap", you will still need to pull your weight. What you get is a fast-track ticket, not a free lunch. With the right attitude, a lot that's exciting awaits you. Be bold, be hungry, be brave!

BUSINESS - *Big opportunities*
A good time to network and to expand your reach. The more you collaborate with others, the quicker you will be able to grow. A time when you can take some risks venturing into new territory. Definitely a gung-ho month when going for gold is the way forward. If you are in search of big success, take advantage of the auspicious energies in your chart.

Things are looking very good, so this is an appropriate month to plan for new things. Taking calculated risks now will bring success and wealth. There are powerful forces at work and things are moving quickly. It is important not to be idle if you want big things to happen for you.

LOVE & RELATIONSHIPS - *In flux*
Your relationship may be in a constant state of flux, and you may see yourself heading to a crossroads. The choices you make now may deepen the bond you share with your partner or they may drive you further apart. This is a volatile month and could see the ending of a relationship if the road you take is too different from that of your partner's.

On the other hand, while you pursue your diverse interests, nothing may change when it comes to your romantic ties. It is difficult to predict what will happen for you except that just about anything can. If you value the union you have with your partner, it is a good idea to work at it this month.

EDUCATION - *Don't overtax yourself*
Because there is so much happening and you cannot participate in everything, you may feel you are missing out. This feeling will pass. It is best to just keep life ticking over. Doing too much may cause you to get overexhausted. There may be a reason you cannot do everything! Focus your pent-up energy on your schoolwork and you could find fulfillment there.

FOURTH MONTH
May 6th - June 5th 2018

Prosperity Star brings rich rewards

Fortune smiles on you, bringing rich rewards to everything you undertake. Although you may face some adversity, these will be minor compared to the highs of the month. All the stars gracing your chart are positive, and so anything you start now are likely to lead to good outcomes. This is a time when you can move firmly forward with any plans you may have. Stop feeling unsure over issues you've had trouble with in the past. Use your confidence to pursue anything you've put on hold because you were too apprehensive before.

A time to follow your dreams. Although you have money, career and wealth luck on your side, they may not be your main concerns. Take time out for yourself to pursue where your heart takes you.

 ## WORK & CAREER
Don't hold grudges

A hassle-free month frees you up to spend time on other areas of your life, although this does not mean you should neglect your career or be non-serious about your work. You have few enemies in the workplace and are well on top of your tasks.

To really enjoy the month, work efficiently and accurately and you will leave yourself enough time to focus some energy into other areas of your life. You may be asked to work with certain individuals you've had issues with in the past. Forget what is past and don't hold grudges. If you act like there is no issue, the other side will as well. You will only gain from working well together, so don't create problems where there are none.

BUSINESS - *Clockwork*
A super month when things seem to run like clockwork, needing you to do very little. You could do even better if you put in more effort, but because you have other things on your mind, making money may not be top of your agenda. You have a devoted and competent staff who can keep things ticking over, leaving you time to pursue other things outside of work. A safe time to invest if you have the urge to do so. Your cash flow is healthy and you can afford to be more decadent when it comes to spending.

LOVE - *Beyond the physical*
The single Sheep will be spoilt for choice if you are looking to get hitched. There may be several suitors waiting in the sidelines. Don't rush into a

relationship unless you are sure it is what you want. Remember that if you get yourself attached to someone, you will not be a free agent when who you really want comes along. Don't hook up jsut because you are feeling a little lonely. Hold out on your heartstrings till you know for sure you have found your soul mate. You may be rather sentimental this month, and you won't be fulfilled unless you can connect with your partner beyond the physical level.

🎓 EDUCATION - *Competitive spirit*

A good time for the young Sheep to learn to work independently. You may be expected to take on a large project on your own. This may be coursework that counts toward your year-end grade or some other important assignment. You will relish the task once you get into it. There is much competitive spirit in you. Use that energy in your schoolwork, but do not let the pressure to do well get to you.

All the hard work you are putting in may cause some to label you a nerd. Look on it as a compliment and let them eat their heart out. You are on a roll, and all the hard work you put in will be worth it once the results come back.

FIFTH MONTH
June 6th - July 6th 2018
Excess of Metal energy brings danger of violence

A volatile month due to an excess of Metal energy. There is risk of burglary, violence and losses. A month to be watchful, whether with personal safety or in business. Do not take risks and do not trust others easily. Betrayal could come from unexpected quarters. Your health may also suffer this month. Try not to over-exert or expose yourself to viruses. Refrain from visiting hospitals, graveyards or attending funerals this month. The yin energy could prove too strong.

FENG SHUI CURE: Elderly Sheep should avoid the SW sector and wear a **Wu Lou** or **Health Amulet** to protect against sickness. You can also wear a **Medicine Buddha** pendant. Do not get yourself involved in fights; there could be tragic consequences. If you feel your blood rising, resist the urge to voice your grievances. Better to walk away.

WORK & CAREER - *Watch your step*
Your professional life may be rather unpredictable. There could be opposing feelings inside you where your career path is concerned, and misunderstandings at the workplace could make you want to throw your hands up in the air and quit. This is not a good time to make reckless decisions that could have a big impact on your future. Calm yourself down by **wearing the colour blue.** This will help quell the destructive stars in your cycle. On the other extreme to those who openly challenge you, there could be hidden enemies waiting for you to make a blunder. Be watchful of your step.

BUSINESS - *Extricate gracefully*
A good idea to keep a close watch on your financials. You may have placed too much trust in someone and been taken for a ride. Carry out routine checks to make sure there is nothing amiss. If you do find something erroneous, don't be too harsh in your confrontations; it could lead to violence. If your losses are small, it may be better to let go. Extricate yourself from partnerships gone wrong gracefully. Avoid showdowns. Deals that have been made without documentation could fall through. Let them be. Don't keep chasing them.

LOVE & RELATIONSHIPS
Third parties

Watch for third parties who could try to make trouble for you in your relationships. If you are happily married, avoid advances that are even remotely sexual in nature. Don't let yourself fall victim to sweet talk. You could end up losing the things most important to you. Jealousy may rear its ugly head and you could find yourself being caught up in a love triangle. Avoid juggling relationships. No matter how well you think you know a person, they can still surprise you. The violent stars are lined up this month and it is important not to trigger anything that could cause an outburst.

EDUCATION - *Get enough rest*

Pay closer attention to details. You may find it difficult to concentrate in class if you've been keeping late nights. Getting enough rest is important for both your health and your progress in school. Because there are danger stars in your chart, it is better to stay at home than to go out too much. On school excursions, be more careful. Do not wander off on your own. Be wary of strangers.

SIXTH MONTH
July 7th - Aug 7th 2018
Exciting new opportunities

Your luck improves bringing plenty of opportunities
your way. You don't even need to look for them, they
are right there in front of you. Obstacles to success
are few and far between, so it is unlikely anything
can crop up to ruin victory for you. However, all
your successes are a direct result of your sweat and
toil. The rewards are forthcoming, but need to be
earned. That also means that whatever good things
come your way are all of your own doing. The other
plus point is that your gains this month will be
long-lasting. This is a time when it benefits you to
take on a mentor figure. Your connections to people
with influence will play a major role in helping you
attain what you set out to achieve. There may be a
phone call or two to make to call on a favour. Don't
be reticent about asking for help when you need it.

WORK & CAREER
Making an impression

You are likely to impress someone who matters.
It could be your direct boss or someone in
management. The positive results of this may not
manifest until later in the year, but the seeds will
have been sown. Someone more senior may take

you under their wing; and this person could grow to become a very important part of your professional life later on. You may be invited to join special project meetings. Embrace the opportunity to work closer with top management, and do as much as you can to learn.

BUSINESS - *Quiet confidence*
You are feeling hands-on and involved in the day-to-day operations of what you are doing. You have plenty of charm in your personality which will give you an edge when facing off the competition. When bidding for projects, do not let yourself get intimidated by the bigwigs. Neither should you allow yourself to come across arrogant. Maintain the right balance of quiet confidence and you will do well. A joint venture with an influential partner may swing things in your favour. Do not drive too hard a bargain. Too much greed now may leave you with nothing.

LOVE & ROMANCE - *Long-term*
This month you can strengthen existing relationships, or if you are single, you may be enjoying the beginnings of a new relationship. Your love life will be more about the long term than on light-hearted romance. You find casual flirting

rather innocuous right now, preferring some form of commitment from your partner. But once you find someone who thinks the way you do, there will be plenty of passion in your union. Some of you may see relationships develop out of friendships. It may not be love at first sight, but you will feel the heat intensify as you move forward in your feelings for each other.

EDUCATION - *Study luck*

You have luck on your side and find yourself popular with the teachers. Your friends may well brand you a teacher's pet, but this will be in good fun and jest. Do not take anything to heart when it is meant as a joke. Spending more effort on your schoolwork will bring more than proportionate results.

FAMILY - *Pearls of wisdom*

The older generation has much to pass on in terms of wisdom. Do not shun the advice of the older folk in the family. This month you should be listening harder! There is a lot to be gained from the lips of an older mentor figure. You may not fully digest what they have to say at first, but somewhere in the future, what you've learned will suddenly dawn on you to be very important indeed.

SEVENTH MONTH
Aug 8th - Sept 7th 2018
Five Yellow put a dampener on plans

Your luck takes a dive with the appearance of the *Five Yellow*. Expect obstacles to surface as soon as you lay down any plans. This month it may be better not to make plans at all, because the mere act of planning could cause those plans to unravel. One of those months when it is better to take each day as it comes. Avoid taking risks, signing or sealing anything. Think of this as a transitory period. Continue to build goodwill with friends and associates but don't commit yourself to anything.

FENG SHUI TIP: Because you have misfortune stars fluttering nearby, it is necessary to protect yourself with **amulets.** Display the **Five Element Pagoda** in the SW of your home. Watch your cash flow. Do not overspend or you could find yourself in a cash bind.

WORK & CAREER - *Lie low*

If you are finding work stressful, make sure you get some balance by spending time outside of work. Use the support your family can give you. Bitch about your boss at home but never let on what you are feeling in front of your colleagues. To show your disgruntled side could prove professional suicide this month. If you are not careful, a sudden outburst could even cost you your job! Focus on keeping yourself under control. Wait for another time if you have ambitions with regard to your job. This month it is better to stay quiet and low key.

BUSINESS - *Roadblocks*

Not a good time to take risks or invest. Delay large capital outlays and conserve your cash. Avoid too much publicity for your business. Projecting the wrong image now could be damaging for your reputation in the long run.

Don't expect too much this month. Consider yourself lucky if things don't slow down for you. This is a dry month when it comes to opportunities. Sales are slower than usual and deals you thought were already sealed could open up again with hitches and problems. There may be a misunderstanding with a business partner over money matters. If the matter can wait till next month to be settled, it is better to wait. You are unlikely to resolve anything now and could end up souring a relationship.

LOVE - *Companionship*

Because your overall luck is poorly, you have little energy left to feel romantic. Your love life will be more of the companionship type than anything too hot. What you will appreciate however is a partner who understands you. This may actually be the best time to get together with someone, for in your current mood, you will know if they are the sort who will stick around for the long haul.

EDUCATION - *Feeling used*

For the young Sheep, unexpected problems may crop up. An argument with a friend, or you may feel betrayed or used. Shrug off those negative feelings and focus on your schoolwork instead. It may be difficult when you have other things on your mind, but mulling over what is past will help nothing.

EIGHTH MONTH
Sept 8th - Oct 7th 2018
Love and relationships blossom

Love luck blossoms for the Sheep. This is a time when you may well find the real thing! There is marriage on the cards, or a serious relationship that could lead to marriage in the future. A lot to smile about! After a difficult month with the *Five Yellow*, the future looks bright once again; but the best aspects of the month will be on the relationship side. You get along much better with others, and if things have been weird between you and a friend, you can repair things this month.

The *#4 Relationship Star* also combines very well with the #6 in your chart to form a *sum-of-ten*. This brings completion luck to all your projects and endeavours, and suggests a wonderful ending to everything you start. It means you can complete things.

 ## WORK & CAREER
Chance encounters

A time when making connections with others will feature strongly. The support of friends and allies becomes invaluable and you may happen on chance encounters that lead to great things later on. The initiative lies with you, so be prepared to make the first move. Call up old friends, or new friends you have just met. Playing an introductory role connecting people will also feature in your work this month. Step outside your official duties. A time when you can impress the boss.

BUSINESS - *Eye-openener*

Luck in business is good. There are many opportunities to seize; all you need to do is be a little courageous and willing to take some risks. When new opportunities present themselves, keep an open mind before making any decisions. Socializing in different circles will suggest new avenues down which you may want to go. There is a lot out there, and this month could feel like a massive eye opener when you get a crash course on everything you have been missing.

Some crucial information may make its way into your orbit, giving you the key to finally unlock something you have been pondering over for a while now. Investment luck is promising. You may be thinking about broadening your scope of business. As long as you feel right about it, be bold pursuing new things. Although wealth luck is good, immediate returns may not be top of your priority.

LOVE & RELATIONSHIPS
Promising

This will be a busy month for the Sheep socially, and while you may be actively looking for romance, your friends take up a lot of your time. Indeed there may be precious little left over for meeting new people or going on a proper date! However, if someone catches your eye, you should not have a problem rearranging your schedule.

Go with the flow. The stars are in alignment to help you. Not only do you have the *Peach Blossom Star* which attracts romantic opportunities, you also enjoy *sum-of-ten* luck, which usually causes results to come, and things to ripen for you.

EDUCATION - *Study luck*

Schoolwork becomes highly enjoyable. The energies of the month bring you study luck, which not only makes it easier to focus on your work but also helps you achieve real accolades when it comes to your studies. A time when you could win scholarships and awards if you put your mind to it.

NINTH MONTH
Oct 8th - Nov 6th 2018
Quarrelsome star causes havoc

The *#3 Argumentative Star* brings conflict into your life. It makes you more unreasonable, causing you to fight even with those who are firmly on your side. When you look back at the aftermath of each quarrel you start, you may wonder what the issue was, but if you are not careful, some things, once said, are difficult to take back. Better to lie low and think hard before you react or say something you regret. A month that resembles a tightrope to walk upon. You may be feeling more insecure than usual and this could cause you to lash out. Avoid revealing your innermost feelings. Choose your confidantes carefully. Some may use your weaknesses against you, while others may get the wrong impression of you.

FENG SHUI TIP: Carry the **Peace & Harmony Amulet**. Display the **Garuda Bird** in your home sector of SW. The #3 star is a Wood Star, and is especially harmful to the Sheep, who is of the Earth element, as Wood destroys Earth.

WORK & CAREER - *Battle of wits*

There may be testing situations to deal with and difficult people to navigate. Watch out for colleagues you may not know well who have reason to make you slip up. It is usually good to think the best of others, but this does not mean you need to trust them. If it comes down to survival of the fittest, you will need to be as cunning as your opponent if you want to emerge victorious. Do not reveal what is on your mind lest you give away too much.

BUSINESS - *Tension*

A tension-filled month. You may have to work out a business deal but find it hard to agree on certain issues. If you can, postpone dealmaking, especially when there is a lot at stake. You may have to overcome opposition to your ideas, especially if you are in a partnership with other parties. The fighting factions come from within the ranks this month.

If you have been used to giving orders and getting what you want, this is a time when your authority could be challenged. Be careful of other equally ambitious people who may appear to want to do you in. It is important to watch your back at a time like this.

LOVE & RELATIONSHIPS
Do not judge

This month may see you questioning your relationships. Avoid falling into the syndrome of making it a competition of who makes more of an effort or who spends more money. Love is not built on being calculative. If you want your relationship to last, you need to consciously stop yourself from judging your partner.

Because the month is filled with quarrelsome energies, you may find much to disagree about. Avoid allowing a silly lover's tiff to become something more serious by letting go of your ego. Make it a rule that if one of you apologizes, the other has to accept the apology.

EDUCATION - *Move on*

You may make some mistakes that get you down. Learn from them but do not dwell on them. If you expend all your energy feeling sorry for yourself, there will be no time to get on with your work and the things that really matter. Mistakes are there to be made so you can learn. You may have to face a few disappointments, but take them in your stride and look forward to a better time next month.

TENTH MONTH
Nov 7th - Dec 6th 2018
Low energy month gets you down

A low energy, high-pressure period looms ahead, with the *Illness Star #2* making its way into your chart. This could cause you feel sluggish with little energy to pursue all the daunting tasks before you. Try to avoid mental overload by planning your schedule well. Include some rest and relaxation time each day. Avoid stressful situations or you could end up a nervous wreck. This is a month when it is best for you to lie low month and refrain from taking on too many additional responsibilities.

WORK & CAREER - *High workload*
A demanding time at work awaits. Your problems stem from the sheer bulk of work you need to complete, or the tasks you are handling may seem particularly difficult. Try to focus on the things that matter most. If you do find yourself tackling something new, be open and ask for help if you need it. Don't bluff your way through. This is a time when you will appreciate having allies at the workplace. Might be a good way to make peace with those you may have had issues with in the past.

BUSINESS - *Arms-length approach*
This may be a worrying month with one problem after the next. While the obstacles you face may be small, your frame of mind is not attuned to coping all that well. Keep as calm and collected as you can, and avoid hasty reactions to problems. Your first response will probably not be the best one. Take time to digest any surprises you face before taking action.

For now, it may be better to take an arms-length approach. Because your personal luck is weak, too much of your input may harm rather than help. If business is going fine as usual, try not to do too much to interfere. This is a bad time to implement new ideas or try new things. The coming month is more conducive to any kind of change, so wait a while before making any major alterations at the workplace.

LOVE & RELATIONSHIPS - *Slow*
Your love life limps awkwardly along mainly because your energy levels are ebbing at their lowest point. Sheep at the early stages of dating will probably lack the energy to put yourselves wholeheartedly with your date. Might be a time to focus on other areas of your life which

are demanding your attention. Those already in a relationship however are likely to find your partner a big source of support. Lean on them, share your worries, it can draw the two of you closer.

EDUCATION - *Swamped*

There may seem more for you to do than usual. More deadlines to meet may run up your stress levels. Make it a point to start your assignments early so you don't find yourself running out of time to complete them. There is no need to be too perfect. Get the work done. Remember, it is better to peak at the right time. You cannot be working at your best all through the year. Keep up a good standard of work, but don't let your health suffer because of it.

HEALTH - *Look after yourself*

Do not take your health for granted; the *Illness Star #2* causes you to fall sick more easily. You are more susceptible to viruses and may find yourself plagued by migraines. If you are feeling under the weather, take it easy. Those who are ill should avoid residing in the SW this month. The #2 also brings increased risk of accidents, so if you partake in dangerous sports, don't take risks this month.

ELEVENTH MONTH
Dec 7th 2018 - Jan 5th 2019
A month for gaining knowledge

An excellent month awaits those of you pursuing knowledge and looking to learn something new! The *#1 Victory Star* joins the #6 to form the *1/6 Ho Tu*, which enhances intelligence and fuels study luck. A great time for the student Sheep. This is also a time of new opportunities. The winds of change are blowing, so you may meet with some unexpected but positive transformations. Go with the flow as destiny has grand plans for you!

Your leadership qualities get enhanced making it a good time for those standing for any kind of election. Sheep in management will find their authority strengthened. There is also improved money luck on the cards. Be open to new ideas. Wealth does not always come in its usual guise. If you are sharp, there are some wonderful opportunities to seize.

WORK & CAREER - *Productive*
You enjoy a productive month at work, particularly if you are in a managerial position. Learn to delegate effectively and organize your team members as a cohesive unit. At an emotional

level, this month will be like the calm after a storm. While last month was all about plenty happening at once, now you can take stock and plan. This is a good time to get new projects off the ground, but they will probably still be in their infancy stage. Do not rush anything. It is better to take things steady for now.

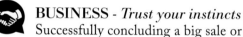

BUSINESS - *Trust your instincts*
Successfully concluding a big sale or contract will keep you busy, and you do well navigating tricky negotiations. Some deals may appear too good to be true but you can afford to have a little faith. Trust your instincts which will serve you well. Do not get anxious about overcommitting yourself. If you have a good team in place, there is a lot you can take on. You are feeling energised. How productive you are depends entirely on your own confidence.

LOVE & RELATIONSHIPS
Future plans
An excellent month for Sheep to get married, get engaged or start a family. Start looking at your path ahead and ensure yours and your partner's can converge if you want to build a future together. Try not to keep secrets from each other. A good time

for heart-to-hearts and open discussions. Engineer deeper conversations if you are serious about taking your relationship to the next level.

For those in dead-end relationships, the time may have come to end things, or change things. If that is the case, have the courage to move on. Or you could just be delaying the inevitable. You are feeling strong this month and will be surprised just how well you can handle any changes that need to happen.

EDUCATION - *Set the bar high*

A truly wonderful time for the student Sheep! The stars are geared towards luck in learning and gaining knowledge. Those taking exams can do very well. Remember to aim high. Don't be content with perfecting what you already know, go further in your quest for knowledge. When you set the bar really high is when you can go further than you ever imagined. Have confidence in your abilities and don't listen to anyone who tries to plant any doubt in your mind.

TWELFTH MONTH
Jan 6th - Feb 3rd 2019
Fast-moving and fulfilling

The *#9 Future Prosperity Star* joins the *Heaven Star #6* to bring more good things into your life. The *Fire Star* fuels your intrinsic element of Earth, giving you an energy boost. You feel optimistic about the month ahead and for good reason. You are on a roll! This is a time to set things up for the future. The year that's coming up quickly brings some tricky moments to navigate, making it doubly important to develop a strong foundation now. Next year, the Sheep has to contend with the *Five Yellow* in its sector. For now, enjoy the auspicious stars in your chart and do what you can to lay the groundwork for what is to come.

 WORK & CAREER - *Clarity*
While it may be a hectic time at work, you experience a newfound clarity. You can see where you are headed, and that gives you a strong sense of security. Some of you may gain a promotion; if this is what you have been working towards, keep focused on this. Gear your actions to ensuring you continue to impress. There are opportunities to get yourself involved in more; don't shy away from taking on more work. When you get on board

with more responsibilities, it will give you access to the bigger picture, which makes your other tasks seem much simpler. Doubling the responsibilities does not mean double the workload - in fact, it will increase your proficiency at your job and your prospects for the future. Adopt a can-do attitude and let the momentum of the month take you to high places in your career.

BUSINESS - *Stay visible*
A good month for raising your profile. Being in the news brings benefits. You have the luck of fame and recognition on your side, making this a good time to engage in greater marketing efforts. The media are on your side so make the most of their interest in you. Stroke the egos of your journalist friends. This month flattery gets you everywhere, so don't be sparing with your compliments! You will be surprised how even the most fawning statements come out sounding real if you know how to deliver them.

Your luck is good so you can invest and expand with confidence. But because you seem to be on a roll, you may tend to act without thinking through all the consequences. Don't be overly impulsive. Use your head when making decisions.

♥ LOVE & RELATIONSHIPS
Passionate

There are numerous opportunities to forget everything else and follow your heart this month. You can afford to do that if you are young, but for those with other responsibilities in life, you may need to make a conscious effort not to neglect them. A deceptive month because you are enjoying some very good stars in your chart. Seize the moment, but watch you don't do anything that could jeopardise what you already have.

🎓 EDUCATION - *Excellent*

Your higher energy levels allow you to take on more. Some of you may have important choices to make; seek the advice of someone wiser if you are unsure. Don't let negative thoughts enter your head, because the thoughts you create will perpetuate themselves into reality. This leads to another point. The friends and company you keep become more important than ever. Don't spend too much time with anyone who does not make you feel good about yourself.

for more on all the recommended
feng shui cures, remedies & enhancers for

2018

please log on to

www.fsmegamall.com/2018